Rock Junction
Essays and short fiction by John Long

Chockstone Press
Evergreen, Colorado

ROCK JUNCTION: ESSAYS AND SHORT FICTION BY JOHN LONG.

ISBN 0-934641-68-4

Published and distributed by:

Chockstone Press, Inc.
Post Office Box 3505
Evergreen, CO 80439

Font cover: John Long at Joshua Tree National Monument. Photo by Kevin Powell.

Although some of the works included here are of an autobiographical nature (*Green Arch, First Time, Don Jesus, Scorched Earth* and *Rats*), some are based in large part on experiences of the author and may use factual locations and personalities in a purely fictitious manner (*Tirada los Tubos, Candles for Ulak, Red Rock* and *Last Place on No Map*). The others exist only in the fevered and turbid imagination of the author and any resemblance to persons living or dead is unintentional and purely coincidental.

To Zachenca, Herlinda, Estela, e Jesus Aguilera, and the loving memory of Ruth Emma Long

Table of Contents

Foreword

The first adventure book I read as a boy was *No Picnic on Mount Kenya* by Felice Benuzzi. An incredibly gripping tale very simply told, the yarn was good enough to keep me enthralled. Adventure books have since become my life's work and passion, and to reproduce the thrill I felt while reading a story such as Benuzzi's is my eternal quest. *Rock Junction* has answered this challenge.

After a legendary climbing career in Yosemite and elsewhere, and numerous adventures in jungles, oceans and rivers, John Long has realized—as did Conrad, London, Hemingway and Chatwin before him—that adventure literature is best written with a proper mix of real experiences and imaginary ones, and the reader is much the richer for the blend. All too often the adventure stories we read are not stories at all, but articles posturing as stories—tedious, predictable and without a signature voice or personality. Not so with *Rock Junction*. From the very first line we know exactly who is writing, and in time, who that writer is.

We tend always to think of the adventures, and Long has many peers in the field. What makes John Long distinctive is the evident skill with which he manipulates language. He is able to weave an intricate story that will take the reader on a harrowing ride from laughing at Long's darkly humorous observations of singular people and exotic locales, to feeling the fire of peril, and finally finding ourselves staring at our own worst fear. This is real fear, not of death in a savage and unimaginable place, but the fear of meeting oneself, or meeting that internal blackness that eclipses any physical threat—an enlightenment through physical endurance. Redemption and self-revelation are as elusive and ominous for Long as surviving the dark current on a nameless jungle river. His writing fits well into the adventure genre, yes; but it is fine psychological literature above all, for Long's stories operate on at least two levels: that which propels the narrative, and that which elevates the reader's awareness in a profound way.

There are precious few good storytellers in the adventure genre today, and I am pleased that John Long has seen fit to add to the world's supply. Since his first collection of stories, *Gorilla Monsoon*, Long has continued to grow as a writer—and with *Rock Junction*, he has in fact, transcended the adventure genre altogether. The reader will find themselves moved by these stories, almost *used* by the stories. And days later you will find yourself still thinking about them.

Michael Chessler
Chessler Books
Kittredge, Colorado
February 22, 1994

It is not down on any map; true places never are.

Herman Melville
Moby Dick

The Green Arch

We came from nowhere towns like Upland, Cucamonga, Ontario, and Montclair. None of us had done anything more distinguished than chase down a fly ball or spend a couple of nights in juvenile hall, but we saw rock climbing as a means to change all that. *Lonely Challenge, The White Spider, Straight Up*—we'd read them all, could recite entire passages by heart. It is impossible to imagine a group more fired up by the romance and glory of the whole climbing business than we were. There was just one minor problem: There were no genuine mountains in Southern California. But there were plenty of rocks. Good ones, too.

Every Saturday morning during the spring of 1972, about a dozen of us would jump into a medley of the finest junkers $200 could buy and blast for the little alpine hamlet of Idyllwild, home of Tahquitz Rock. The last twenty-six miles to Idyllwild is a twisting road, steep and perilous in spots. More than one exhausted Volkswagen bus or wheezing old Rambler got pushed a little too hard, blew up and was abandoned, the plates stripped off and the driver, laden with rope and pack, thumbing on toward Mecca. We had to get to a certain greasy spoon by eight o'clock, when our little group, the Stonemasters, would meet, discuss an itinerary, wolf down some food and storm off to the crags with all the subtlety of a spring hailstorm.

The air was charged because we were on a roll, our faith and gusto growing with each new climb we bagged. The talk within the climbing community was that we were crazy, or liars, or both; and this sat well with us. We were loud-mouthed eighteen-year-old punks, and proud of it.

Tahquitz was one of America's hot climbing spots, with a pageant of pivotal ascents reaching back to when technical climbing first came to the States. America's first 5.8 (The Mechanic's Route) and 5.9 (The Open Book) routes were bagged at Tahquitz, as was the notion and the deed of the "first free ascent," a route first done with aid but later climbed without it (The Piton Pooper, 5.7, circa 1946). John Mendenhall, Chuck Wilts, Mark Powell, Royal Robbins, Tom Frost, TM Herbert, Yvon Chouinard, Bob Kamps and many others had all learned the ropes there.

The Stonemasters arrived on the scene about the same time that the previous generation of local hard cores—a smug, high-blown group of would-be photographers and assistant professors—was being overtaken by house payments and squealing brats. They hated every one of us. We were all ninety cents away from having a buck, ragged as roaches, eating the holes out of doughnuts—and we cared nothing for their endorsement. We'd grappled up many of their tougher climbs, not with grace, but with pure gumption and fire, and the limelight was panning our way.

The old guard was confounded that we of so little talent and experience should get so far. When it became common knowledge that we were taking a bead on the hallowed Valhalla (one of the first 5.11 routes in America)—often tried, but as yet unrepeated—they showed their teeth. If we so much as dreamed of climbing Valhalla, we'd have to wake up and apologize. The gauntlet was thus thrown down: If they wouldn't hand over the standard, we'd rip it from their hands. When, after another month, we all had climbed Valhalla, some of us several times, the old boys were stunned and saw themselves elbowed out of the opera house by kids who could merely scream. And none could scream louder than Tobin Sorenson, the most conspicuous madman to ever lace up Varappes.

Climbing had never seen the likes of Tobin, and probably never will again. He had the body of a welterweight, a lick of sandy brown hair and the faraway gaze of the born maniac; yet he lived with all the precocity and innocence of a child. He would never cuss or show the slightest hostility; around girls he was so shy he'd flush and stammer. But out on the sharp end of the rope he was a fiend in human form. Over the previous summer he'd logged an unprecedented string of gigantic falls that should have ended his career, and his life, ten times over. Yet he shook each fall off and clawed straight back onto the route for another go, and usually got it. He became a world-class climber very quickly.

He was so well formed and savagely motivated that we knew he would gain the top in no time—if he didn't kill himself first. When we started bagging new climbs and first free ascents, Tobin continued to defy the gods with his electrifying peelers. The exploits of his short life deserve a book. Two books.

One Saturday morning, five or six of us hunkered down in our little restaurant in Idyllwild. Tahquitz was our oyster. We'd pried it open with a piton and for months had gorged at will; but the fare was running thin. Since we had ticked off one after another of the remaining new routes, our options had dwindled to only the most grim or preposterous. During the previous week, Ricky Accomazzo had scoped out the Green Arch, an elegant arc on Tahquitz's southern shoulder. When Ricky mentioned he thought there was an outside chance that this pearl of an aid climb might go free, Tobin looked like the Hound of the Baskervilles had just heard the word "bone," and we had to lash him to the booth so we could finish our oatmeal.

Since the Green Arch was Ricky's idea, he got the first go at it. Tobin balked, so we tied him off to a stunted pine and Ricky started up. After fifty feet of dicey wall climbing, he gained the arch, which soared above for another eighty feet before curving right and disappearing in a field of big knobs and pockets. If we could only get to those knobs, the remaining 300 feet would go easily and the Green Arch would fall. But the lower corner and the arch above looked bleak. The crack in the back of the arch was too thin to accept even fingertips, and both sides of the corner were blank and marble-smooth. By pasting half his rump on one side of the puny corner, and splaying his feet out on the opposite side, Ricky stuck to the rock—barely—both his arse and his boots steadily oozing off the steep, greasy wall. It was exhausting duty just staying put, and moving up was accomplished in a grueling, precarious sequence of quarter-inch moves. Amazingly, Ricky jackknifed about halfway up the arch before his calves pumped out. He lowered off a bunk piton and I took a shot.

After an hour of the hardest climbing I'd ever done, I reached a rest hold just below the point where the arch swept out right and melted into that field of knobs. Twenty feet to paydirt. But those twenty feet didn't look promising.

There were some sucker knobs just above the arch, but those ran out after about twenty-five feet and would leave a climber in the bleakest no-man's land, with nowhere to go, no chance to climb back right onto the route, no chance to get any protection, and no chance to retreat. We'd have to stick to the arch.

Finally, I underclung about ten feet out the arch, whacked in a suspect knifeblade piton, clipped the rope in—and fell off. I lowered to the ground, slumped back, and didn't rise for ten minutes. I had weeping strawberries on both ass cheeks, and my ankles were rubbery and tweaked from splaying them out on the far wall.

Tobin, unchained from the pine, tied into the lead rope and stormed up the corner like a man fleeing Satan on foot. He battled up to the rest hold, drew a few quick breaths, underclung out to that creaky, buckled, driven-straight-up-into-an-expanding-flake knifeblade, and immediately cranked himself over the arch and started heaving up the line of sucker knobs.

"No!" I screamed up. "Those knobs don't go anywhere!" But it was too late.

Understand that Tobin was a born-again Christian, that he'd smuggled Bibles into Bulgaria risking twenty-five years on a Balkan rockpile, that he'd studied God at a fundamentalist university, and none of this altered the indisputable fact that he was perfectly mad. Out on the sharp end he not only ignored all consequences, but actually loathed them, doing all kinds of crazy, incomprehensible things to mock them. (The following year, out at Joshua Tree, Tobin followed a difficult, overhanging crack with a rope noosed around his neck.) Most horrifying was his disastrous capacity to simply charge at a climb pell mell. On straightforward routes, no one was better. But when patience and cunning were required, no one was worse. Climbing, as it were, with blinders on, Tobin would sometimes claw his way into the most grievous jams. When he'd dead end, with nowhere to go and looking at a Homeric peeler, the full impact of his folly would hit him like a wrecking ball. He would panic, wail, weep openly, and do the most ludicrous things. And sure enough, about twenty-five feet above the arch those sucker knobs ran out, and Tobin had nowhere to go.

To appreciate Tobin's quandary, understand that he was twenty-five feet above the last piton, which meant he was looking at a fifty-foot fall, since a leader falls twice as far as he is above the last piece of protection. The belayer (the man tending the other end of the rope) cannot take in rope during a fall because it happens too fast. He can only secure the rope—lock it off. But the gravest news was that I knew the piton I'd bashed under the roof would not hold a fifty-foot whopper. On really gigantic falls, the top piece often rips out, but the fall is broken sufficiently for a lower piece to stop you. In Tobin's case, the next lower piece was some dozen feet below the top one, at the rest hold, so in fact, Tobin was looking at close to an eighty-footer—maybe more with rope stretch.

As Tobin wobbled far overhead, who should lumber up to our little group but his very father, a minister, a quiet, retiring, imperturbable gentleman who hacked and huffed from his long march up to the cliffside. After hearing so much about climbing from Tobin, he'd finally come to see his son in action. He couldn't have shown up at a worse time. It was like a page from a B-movie script—us cringing and digging in, waiting for the bomb to drop; the good pastor, wheezing through his moustaches, sweat-soaked and confused, squinting up at the fruit of his loins; and Tobin, knees knocking like castanets, sobbing pitifully and looking to plunge off at any second.

There is always something you can do, even in the grimmest situation, if only you keep your nerve. But Tobin was gone, totally gone, so mastered by terror that he seemed willing to die to be rid of it. He glanced down. His face was a study. Suddenly he screamed, "Watch me! I'm gonna jump."

We didn't immediately understand what he meant.

"Jump off?" Richard yelled.

"Yes!" Tobin wailed.

"NO!" we all screamed in unison.

"You can do it, son!" the pastor put in.

Pop was just trying to put a good face on it, God bless him, but his was the worst possible advice because there was no way Tobin could do it. Or anybody could do it. There were no holds! But inspired by his father's urging, Tobin reached out for those knobs so very far to his right, now lunging, now hopelessly pawing the air.

And then he was off. The top piton shot out and Tobin shot off into the grandest fall I've ever seen a climber take and walk away from—a spectacular, tumbling whistler. His arms flailed like a rag doll's, and his scream could have frozen brandy. Luckily, the lower piton held and he finally jolted onto the rope, hanging upside down and moaning softly. We slowly lowered him off and he lay motionless on the ground and nobody moved or spoke or even breathed. You could have heard a pine needle hit the deck. Tobin was peppered with abrasions and had a lump the size of a pot roast over one eye. He lay dead still for a moment longer, then wobbled to his feet and shuddered like an old cur crawling from a creek. "I'll get it next time," he grumbled.

"There ain't gonna be no next time!" said Richard.

"Give the boy a chance," the pastor threw in, thumping Tobin on the back.

When a father can watch his son pitch eighty feet down a vertical cliff, and straightaway argue that we were short changing the boy by not letting him climb back up and have a second chance at an even longer whistler, we knew the man was mad, and that there was no reasoning with him. But the fall had taken the air out of the whole venture, and we were through for the day. The "next time" came four years later. In one of the most famous leads of that era, Ricky flashed the entire arch on his first try. Tobin and I followed.

Tobin would go on to solo the north face of the Matterhorn, the Walker Spur and the Shroud on the Grandes Jorasses (all in Levis), would make the first alpine ascent of the Harlin Direct on the Eiger, the first ascent of the Super Couloir on the Dru, would repeat the hardest free climbs and big walls in Yosemite, and would sink his teeth into the Himalaya. He was arguably the world's most versatile climber during the late 1970s. But nothing really changed: He always climbed as if time were too short for him, pumping all the disquietude, anxiety, and nervous waste of a normal year into each route.

I've seen a bit of the world since those early days at Tahquitz, have done my share of crazy things, and have seen humanity with all the bark on, primal and raw. But I've never since experienced the electricity of watching Tobin out there on the very quick of the long plank, clawing for the promised land. He finally found it in 1980, attempting a solo ascent of Mt. Alberta's north face. His death was a tragedy, of course. Yet I sometimes wonder if God Himself could no longer bear the strain of watching Tobin wobbling and lunging way out there on the sharp end of the rope, and finally just drew him into the fold.

Don Jesus

T hrough rags of shifting clouds we caught glimpses of a great cascade plunging past an orange wall and spreading into a billowing bridal veil at the boulder-strewn base, 3,212 feet below: Angel Falls, the world's largest. In two days, for network television cameras, Jim Bridwell and I were to rappel down the rock wall just next to the gusher. The assignment looked different than I'd imagined back in Los Angeles.

The creaky D9 transport plane rattled into a thundershower, but quickly burst free into clear air space. The great Venezuelan rain forest stretched into the measureless horizon. Shortly, we skimmed over a copper lake, jounced along a lumpy dirt airstrip and deplaned in Canaima, waving through curtains of flying ants that follow every rain.

Canaima was no "jungle resort," rather a smattering of rustic cabins, a small cafeteria and a gigantic, open air bar on the shore of the lake. Pamon Indians, short and bronzed, with guarded, feral eyes, ran the place—cooked the food, cleaned the rooms, kept the books.

According to Baltazar, a production manager based in Caracas, Pamons had lived around the lake for centuries, and their position in the heart of the rain forest was so remote that they hadn't encountered outsiders until shortly after World War II. Diamonds were found on surrounding rock outcrops, and soon thereafter, every able-bodied Pamon male was sweating his breechcloth off at three flourishing mines. A few Pamon elders, however, played a more crucial role than mere laborers.

Over the generations, the Pamons had developed systematic rituals to interpret the tempestuous elements. Their very survival depended on it, for one glance at Canaima's rotting, proliferating, monstrously exaggerated botany and you'd understand how a small seed, planted in the fecund peat, could swell to a three-kilo melon in a matter of weeks; and conversely, how a relentless monsoon could flood the entire village in a matter of hours. It followed that the antique art of divining storms would be used to the diamond miners' advantage; and there are stories still told of how the mines were constructed and worked in spurts between tortuous rains, as foretold by Pamon shaman.

The mines are played out now, and monsoon-proof cinder block-and-steel dwellings have long replaced the poetic reed huts. Grandsons of the old shaman are presently turned out in pressed Levis and Ray Bans, dancing to "Las Chicas del Can" in the bar. As far as we could tell, time and "progress" had completely severed the charmed alliance these people once had with their milieu.

The next morning Jim and I helicoptered back up to the falls to scout things. Following a ten-minute downpour, we were dismayed to see the gusher surge threefold almost instantly, a perfect torrent plunging down our proposed line of descent. Back in Canaima we asked Baltazar about weather reports. He laughed. They didn't even have a shortwave radio in Canaima. But there was another fascinating option—Don Jesus, the last savant of the old knowledge. We sighed, but Baltazar insisted that while the shaman was a relic even among his own people, the pilots (flying by the seat of their thin pants, with no hard info about the surrounding weather save for what they could see) listened to the old man closely indeed because Don Jesus could "read the rain," or so swore Baltazar.

"Why not?" Jim said. We gave Baltazar twenty Bolivars (roughly five dollars) for Don Jesus' fee, and a little mestizo boy took the money and set off for the Indian's hut. I figured if nothing else, the old man's prediction would have decades of local living behind it.

Shortly, the kid returned, and Jim and I followed him down a dark muddy path that rambled along the margin of the copper lake. The trail veered into the bush to a medley of bamboo and rattan huts. We stopped at the biggest one. Clusters of heliotrope hung in festoons from old tires by the open door, and a screeching spider monkey, tethered to a rusted tractor rim, nearly choked itself trying to get at Jim. We ducked inside.

Don Jesus was a lanky, pulled-out specimen with a face like Methuselah's grandfather—weathered, serene, religious. Thin as a blowgun, his eyes were dark and grave. He sat on a small stool, we on the reed floor. Aside from a sputtering Coleman lantern and a portrait of La Virgin del Coromoto hanging on the wall, the hut was empty.

I explained in Spanish that tomorrow we had to go down Angel Falls on a big rope, that it would take many dangerous hours to do so and if it rained too much, the falls could swell and possibly drown us. We really needed to know about tomorrow's skies.

I was surprised that I could squat there in a vermin filled hut in central nowhere, asking a withered old Indian to divine the weather for us—and really mean it. But the presence of the man, solemn and steady as Father Time, brought a certain greatness to the scene, and seemed to hurl us back to an age when simple questions had simple answers, and when an entire culture hung in the balance with the precision of these answers.

Don Jesus nodded toward a wide leaf at his feet, upon which lay a small mound of whitish powder—chopo, a plant mixture said to be fatal to a common man and to drive dogs mad. The young mestizo scooped a tiny portion into the end of a three-foot bamboo shaft. Don Jesus held the business end to his nose; at the other end, the kid blew the dose up the shaft and deep into Don Jesus. He slouched back, tears streaming down his face, his eyes waxing to infinity. Slowly, he slipped into a sort of waking dream, and took up a small wooden sleeve, elaborately carved and smudged by generations of hands and smoke.

With a flick of the wrist, he tossed out several straight twigs, and for some minutes studied their position on the floor. Only later would I understand that this first toss concerned spatial matters: Somewhere in that tangle of twigs was Angel Falls. The second toss involved the weather, which he divined in seconds. The third toss, which he lingered over with stony enchantment, concerned time: When any clouds should break. The last toss concerned our suerte, or luck.

Throughout, I was struck not by a sense of black artifice or native hooey, but rather how natural the whole business seemed. The old man had thrown those sticks into an intermediate zone where chance and fact converged. Somewhere, traced in the shadow of those sticks lay our future, plain as water—if you were on speaking terms with sun and sky and God. Four tosses, four modalities intertwined tight as the reed walls. Nothing strange about it.

Since the chopo, it seemed as though his spirit, abandoning his body, had wandered to faraway places; but when he looked up, Don Jesus was right back with the living again.

"If you hurry tomorrow, you should be fine," he said. "But any delay and things will turn grave."

"How grave?" I asked.

"That depends on your luck," he said, smiling slightly. And the mestizo kid led us away.

By seven the next morning, Jim and I had thrown a rope over the brink of the world's largest waterfall and were ready to hurry down; but by the time dozens of cameramen were helicoptered into position, it was early afternoon and the skies were slate gray and snarling. An hour later and 1,000 feet below, the clouds cut loose. We were in a fine mess. The wall was so overhanging, we sometimes were dangling many feet out in space above an emptiness big as the sky. One of the 600-foot lines got remarkably tangled, and took Jim an hour to sort out. Some strange jungle reptile, very green and very barbed, worked its way into Jim's shirt, and he nearly pummeled himself to death trying to get it out. The rain hammered down, then fog moved in so thick we could barely see fifty feet. We frantically rappelled down the soaking line. The falls swelled by the minute and now, were thundering only feet away. Finally they washed over us like a glacial blast and, dangling on an 11 millimeter rope, spinning in midair some 2,000 feet above the jungle, we knew we were finished. Had a harsh wind not blown the gusher away from us, we'd still be hanging on that rope. Five hours after starting, we finally touched down—

soaked, freezing, covered in green slime and played all the way out. We dove into the last copter heading south.

We spent two hours grinding through fog and thunder and jet black night. We got lost. Twice. When we finally clanked into Canaima we were running on fumes, and slammed down on to the helipad so hard we broke a skid.

Later that night, as the fifty-man production crew danced to El Tigre the Magnificent and swilled bottle after bottle of raw cane liquor, I made my way back to Don Jesus' hut, and told him what had happened. As the old shaman nodded his head slightly and gently fingered the carved wooden sleeve, I had the exhilarating feeling that I'd taken a ride on that funky velvet chair in H.G. Wells' *Time Machine*, and was again part of something strange and wonderful and old as rain itself.

"I told you to hurry," Don Jesus finally said, "Because it is easier to walk the dry path than the muddy one. But it did not matter so much because the sticks told me you were lucky."

Scorched Earth

F or two days our situation was critical. Then it got desperate. Our teammates were far ahead, and we needed them.
That morning, Rick had been dizzy and hiking slowly, so
we'd sent the others on because we were a week late in finding
the next village. No one could have guessed that an hour after
they had left us, Rick's symptoms would worsen from dizziness
and chills to vomiting and delirium. I pulled him to his feet and
we staggered on, wishing we'd never heard of Borneo, of the
jungle, of any of it.

We wound through the contours of a luxuriant ravine.
Proboscis monkeys screeched high overhead as orange birds shot
between towering banyans. The canopy thickened with each
step, screening the hot rain that fell in a misty curtain through
the hazy green light. The humidity was so thick we exhaled
absolute fog. Recent quakes had triggered landslides throughout
the rolling terrain, and twice we forded steaming tongues of red
mud that flowed over the trail—hip-deep at times—to pick up the
track farther on.

Rick Ridgeway and I were two members of a six-man team
attempting the first coast-to-coast traverse of Kalimantan, or
Indonesian Borneo, a place that time—and everything else—had
forgotten, where our native Dyak porters lived as their ancestors
had centuries ago. We were thirty-two days out—about halfway
across, we hoped, though the government topographic maps
showed a huge blank in the jungled interior. I couldn't imagine a
lonelier place to get sick.

Rick slumped back on a clump of cane leaves and I bashed down to a little creek to get water, wondering what could have so quickly reduced a veteran of K2 and Everest to a shaking, staggering ruin. Dengue, perhaps. Three years before, in the Solomon Islands, I'd seen an entire German sea-kayaking group with dengue fever. It'd resembled a scene from *Night of the Living Dead*. I hoped I was wrong about Rick, but what else could make a man shake like that?

Since leaving the swift Bonai river five days back, we'd thrashed from one Dyak village to the next, linking them with the help of Dyak porters from the former settlement. Most "villages" were no more than clusters of thatched lean-tos, abandoned when the rains stopped and hellacious heat drove the natives into cooler jungle nooks. The next village—Mahak—was supposedly a large one. We couldn't find it. None of our porters had ever been there. But that morning, we'd encountered a band of nomadic Punan Dyaks who said we should have gained Mahak fifteen miles ago.

We continued through the mud, the thorns, the wasps and the leeches. For Rick, staggering through the creepers with a raging fever, every step was a mile. Late that afternoon I wondered if we weren't groping around in a big, tangled circle.

As we broke into a slash-and-burn agricultural swath hacked from a square mile of primal bush, it grew so smoky we could barely see fifty feet. The fuming expanse looked like Hell with the flames turned low. All flora had been felled and torched, to be cleared later for rice fields. Ironwood trees burn slowly, so the blaze lasts for months—never a raging forest fire, but never quite out. The air, thick and suffocating, was so hot it seemed the very sky was melting. A world-class mountaineer, Rick knew about adversity, but heat, smoke and exhaustion had boosted his fever, and he collapsed at the edge of the clearing.

I winced at the thought of bivouacking and started pacing. Then I found a note tacked on a cannonball tree at trail's edge. The rest of the team, the message ran, had met a Dyak from Mahak who assured them the village was only an hour away. Though wasted from the previous twenty miles, they had pressed on, urging us to follow before nightfall. The red sun hung just above the trees like an open wound. We didn't have much time. The only trail wound straight into the smoke.

During the past four hours, Rick had managed to stumble only a hundred yards at a go, shaking, retching and wheezing. I knew we somehow had to get on with it or the whole, crazy safari was going to end for him right there. I told him this, and he instantly struggled to his feet, ready to march on. I had no idea how far he could go, but I couldn't consider getting stranded in the oven before us. We had to push on.

The trail was distinct for a hundred yards. Then the terrain started rolling, and the path disappeared. The only possible route followed a slanting and broken chain of big trunks spanning a sea of red-hot coals. My eyes streamed from the smoke and my nose filled with the copper stench of hair singeing off my legs. The setting sun cloaked the clearing in an orange veil, and the course grew doubly confusing. We couldn't pause, even for a second, without burning our feet through our boots. The temperature soared and the chain of trunks rose higher above the ground, more disconnected, yet overlaid with wobbly charred saplings that might be the way. And might not. Rick was dead on his feet, but continued to worm on. He had to. Blue flames leapt from the gutted ironwood trunks that surrounded us. My body poured sweat and I struggled with the urge to ditch Rick and run for my life. But run where? I wondered what the others had done, what route they had followed.

Just ahead, a fifty-foot smoldering ramin trunk—charred halfway through—bowed across a channel of waist-deep coals. The air rippled from the heat rushing off the red embers. We couldn't stop and we couldn't turn back, so I cast off before I analyzed things, my eyes riveted on the far end of that narrow trunk, shimmering in the smoke. About halfway out, the trunk shifted ever so slightly. My hands shot out for balance and sweat popped off the coals below. For a moment I froze, waiting for the trunk to settle in. There was no way I would fall off, but if the bastard snapped, I was gone. Breathing hot short breaths, I tiptoed on until just shy of the cantilevered end. The trunk made a sharp cracking sound. I panicked, lurched forward and sprung off the end onto a hot and slanting knoll.

I kept shifting from one foot to the other, feeling wretched for having led Rick into no-man's land. I couldn't imagine him traversing that trunk, not in his shape. As he had on so much of this torturous, jackass, extraordinary expedition, he'd have to try because he had no choice. I could hear his reedy breathing from fifty feet away. I thought about going back and helping him, but the trunk was too thin and too charred. We traded sorry looks. He started across.

Arms flailing, he looked like a drunk on a balance beam, but his feet kept shuffling along. Then the trunk started making horrible cracking sounds, and Rick's feet started skating all over the place. I looked away because I couldn't watch him pitch into the coals, twenty feet below him. When I finally looked back, he was close to the end. But he started getting woozy, sucking each breath and looking bone-white and finished. He'd extend his foot like an antenna, rock onto it, wobble, then repeat the move again. I was gnashing my teeth and yelling, "Steady, man, you've got it," fully expecting him to plummet. He wobbled the last few steps and I screamed, "Jump, man, you've got to jump!" But it wasn't in him. He grimaced, groaned, then half-fell, half-hopped toward me. I grabbed his arm, pulled and we tumbled back, rolling up with big watery blisters on our arms and legs.

Rick draped both arms over my shoulders and I plowed through shallow embers to the edge of the fire, a hundred feet beyond. Amazingly, we straightaway ran into a little creek. I toppled in and drank with huge, savage gulps. Then I laid my head on the bank and went out for awhile. When I came around, rain beat down from one black cloud, the blood red moon beside it. A great steamy nimbus welled off the clearing just behind us.

Rick, at the brink of human endurance, still wanted to push on, to get it over with. His fever had first struck while dragging dugout canoes up shallow white water, five days back. Since then, he'd fought through two twelve-hour jungle tromps. And now it was dark and pouring and he wanted to push on. I couldn't figure out what kept him going. Probably Mahak, which we thought had to be close.

It was not.

The squall passed after another hour and we trudged a half-hour through stalks of steaming sugarcane that edged the dark trail, now lit by the moon and the swarms of fireflies that follow every rain. We'd been going for sixteen hours. We stopped. Rick breathed in hideous gasps. Whatever had him, had him good.

Off again. We rounded a corner and there it was: A 600-foot longhouse with dozens of natives huddled around our teammates on the veranda. Everyone had burns and blisters. Yet everyone jumped up and helped Rick into the Chief's rooms. Clad only in briefs, his mouth a blood-bin of betel nut, the Chief rolled out a rattan mat and Rick collapsed. We tried to rehydrate him, but nothing would stay down and we were helpless to do anything but watch him writhe at our feet, more dead than alive. As fluids ebbed out of him from both ends, his limbs slowly enfolded and his torso curled into a shriveled fetal form terrible to witness. His hours were numbered, and we were astounded to hear that Mahak had a seldom-used grass airstrip and that a missionary pilot from the coast was scheduled to visit the next day. The Chief warned that, though the missionary pilot's word was gold, his puny, single-engined Cessna was often thwarted by coastal squalls.

The plane's echo volleyed through the haze the next morning. Rick, a mere wraith by now, was given priority over sacks of rice and sugar, and the missionary volunteered to take him to his home, since there were no proper hospitals, even on the coast. But the oil companies maintained clinics which, the pilot believed, would accept outsiders with green money. We bid Rick goodbye, and as he arced into the clouds, we were left hanging. None of us really believed he was going to make it. Were we next?

For thirty-two days we had motored up the Kapaus river, slow and wide, had bashed and poled up a tributary, swift and rocky, had slashed over the continental divide, an incomprehensible brawl of ripe, primal jungle, had tracked another river and literally dragged the dugouts up its last reaches, only to wander around triple canopy jungle for days before finally gaining Mahak. That worked out to about 500 miles as the crow flies; but with all the tortured paths and twisting rivers, we figured to have covered roughly three times that distance. From Mahak, we reckoned the worse was behind us, for only a relatively brief march separated us from the headwaters of the Kayan river and a straight shot to the coast, 200 miles away.

The "brief" march to the Kayan took a week and covered the toughest terrain we'd encountered. The Kayan ran smooth for a hundred miles, then narrowed to a fleet gauntlet of raging white water we finally had to quit after flipping twice and loosing one raft altogether. Twenty-one days after leaving Mahak, we were back in the jungle for an eighteen-mile hump around suicidal rapids, starving and punctured, our ribs standing out like keys on a xylophone. Once out from under the dense canopy of trees and barbed vines, the sun fried us alive as we charged down steaming white water below the portage.

Tanjun Sellor, the first civilized settlement we'd seen in months, looked like El Dorado but for the equatorial swelter. Christ, how could people live in such stupefying heat? But they were there, dozens of them teeming around the creaky bamboo dock; and amongst the chocolate natives we couldn't mistake Rick's face, shriveled and sallow, but alive. As our little neoprene raft banged into the pylons, we reached out to make sure he was real. He recounted his ghastly hallucinations, how his toes curled and his skin wrinkled like parchment from dehydration. The vein in the crease of his arm was still black and blue from the massive I.V.s he'd needed in his life-and-death struggle with, not dengue, but typhoid and malaria.

The next day, we gained the east coast of Kalimantan and dined with the missionaries that had seen Rick through. While we marveled at the clockwork of chance that had delivered Rick intact, the missionaries wrote the whole thing off to divine intervention, which sounded marvelous.

Borneo was a magical and monstrous land, but we had to get the hell out of there, and fast—to the Tetons, to Glacier National Park, to the North Pole if need be. Somewhere, anywhere that was cold.

Tirada los Tubos

I had packed up and headed back to Venezuela. Solomon's Army couldn't handle the work I had a month to finish, but I went anyway. Mariana planned to flee her teaching job in the phoneless jungle for a week to visit friends and family in El Tigre, her home town. If I didn't join her, brother Luis Manuel would pistol whip me on my next visit.

I hooked up with Mariana in Maracaibo, and also Jimmy, her cousin. Jimmy and I had attended college together in the states, and during spring break of our senior year I'd gone down to Venezuela with him, and had met Mariana. Jimmy had a master's degree in computer science and some fancy government job, but his greater capacity was for knavery and plenty of it. A sworn coward, he nonetheless seemed always to find himself in the middle of impossible adventures and intrigues—with governor's wives; with truculent Yajiros, the local Indians; on jungle canoe trips that always got lost, one for forty-six days. Jimmy Cepeda was God's original fool, and the best friend I ever had.

We piled into Jimmy's van and after a marathon drive, finally wheeled into El Tigre, a blistering savannah peppered with mint thickets, mapora palms and churning oil rigs. Many "Yanqui" engineers hole up here in vast, hermetically sealed campamientos from which they never leave save to go to the airport. The mercury sizzled at ninety-seven in the shade, if you could find any.

The cement house went wild when we arrived. Three-hundred pound Grandmama stopped kneading the arepa and quavered to her feet. Niece Pepina, six-foot-one and thin as a caco quill, dashed over with a tray of pigs feet al carbon as a dozen kids sprang from shady nooks. A Latin home is rarely in want of kids. The people pride themselves on getting married when they want, not when they should, and they're quick to fashion a couple niños because they can. Three years before, I'd been the first gringo to enter their house, or their neighborhood, but so long as I was Jimmy's friend—and now Mariana's fiancé—the house, and everything in it, was mine.

Brother Luis Manuel rushed in, ten-gallon hat perched just above his dark eyes and foot-long pistola in his hand. A thick, mustachioed thirty-five year old with the face of a hangman, he worked sixty-hour-a-week shifts at the petro-chemical plant outside El Tigrito to maintain the dignity of the house. He bolted past Jimmy and I into the jardin to fire three glorious rounds into the sky. Then he laid down a few creole dance steps, booted a sleeping dog, cracked his bullwhip, fired a fourth shot into a stump, and slapped my back till I gasped. His black eyes narrowed:

"Matrimonio? Cuando?"

When I mentioned a very tentative date for the wedding, Luis Manuel's eyes fired like cannons. He kissed Mariana, then me, then Pepina, then Jimmy, then Grandmama, then he broke back into his dancing, faster this time. He made for his pistol but was halted by a bottle of Cacique proffered in Grandmama's plump hand. He'd swilled four fingers before Pepina snatched it back for Grandmama to lock in a chipped wooden cabinet to which there was only one key—the silver skeleton Grandmama that tucked back into her black lace brassiere, a fallow acre no man sober or drunk would dare trespass.

We all sat down and feasted through kilos of bisteak, fried plantains, ensalada aguacate, crunchy sheets of casabe, quarts of jugo de tamarindo and various colorful sweet tubers whose names I could never get my tongue around; and I slowly reentered the emphatic world of a people which, candid and open as the savannah, lived like everybody would if they could stop worrying about life and start living it.

Later, Grandmama got a headache. That prompted a trip to the pharmacia for headache medication, an expedition of exactly three blocks. Luis Manuel could have walked there and back in six minutes, but he took the pickup—because he had one, because it had a full tank, because he'd washed and waxed it earlier that day, and because it had straight pipes and when he gunned it, which he normally did, it sounded like Krakatoa erupting in spurts. All this made the man seem more magnificent as he thundered down the street to the cheers and jeers of friends lounging in thresholds and in hammocks on their verandas. Luis would not travel alone, because going to the pharmacia in the pickup was an event, and an event in Venezuela, no matter how big or how small, is always performed in numbers.

I wedged myself into the bed of the pickup among thirteen kids, four dogs and Grandmama, who Luis Manuel, Jimmy and I had conveyed there in an easy chair, and who would check the date on the medication to ensure it was bueno. As Luis gunned the truck down the road, frame sagging to the pavement, the great straight pipes blasted three-foot flames and whoops roared from every house we passed.

Back in the house, as I watched a red gecko creep across a peeling whitewashed wall, Luis Manuel laid out his plan. Or started to.

"Ave Maria Purisima! What now?" Jimmy laughed. Later, he would explain to me about Luis' "plans," epics that always had him fearing for his life, and which he could never refuse. Most memorable had been bulldogging range donkeys, a stunt that cost Luis Manuel several teeth and a fractured collarbone.

"Tirado los tubos!" Luis said.

"Shooting the tubes?" Jimmy asked.

"Si, chamo," said Luis Manuel. Then he explained.

During construction of the nearly completed hydro-electric plant in Tascabana, thirty miles out of town, the Carina Indians had discovered tube-shooting through accident. The plant's cooling system required re-routing all the surrounding rivers. This was accomplished with five-foot diameter steel tubes that piped water along a twisting route to a central aqueduct. "Tirada los tubos" was to intentionally do what had accidentally happened to a young Indian boy who, while diving for crayfish, got drawn into one of the half-filled drainage tubes. He became a human torpedo, speeding in a black, downhill passage for hundreds of yards before his free-fall exit into the deep aqueduct.

So that we could get a clear picture, Luis Manuel assumed various dive-bomb positions on the cement floor until he spotted a terrific cucaracha on yonder wall—a three-incher, black as sin. He sprang for his bullwhip, but Pepina thrust her pool-cue leg out and tripped him. The roach zipped into a chink in the wall beyond the lunging boys, and the roof nearly blew off for all the laughing, particularly that of Grandmama, who then farted like a tent ripping. At this, she howled so hard the key to the liquor cabinet clinked from her dress. Luis Manuel dove for it, but got only a handful of Pepina's moccasin. Grandmama repositioned the key back in no-man's land, then broke wind again, and we all just had to clear the hell out.

Luis Manuel fanned himself with his hat, and spit for effect, grieving that the next day would mark the end of tube shooting. They were to weld grates over the tubes' entrances when the plant fired up on Monday. The chickens were roosting. The dog had fled to Ecuador. And we were out of beer. Luis Manuel grabbed his bullwhip to look for cockroaches.

We headed out for Tascabana and the tubes early the next morning, rumbling through a scattering of drowsy pueblos. On the outskirts of Rocas Negras, population fifty-six, I saw an adobe shack topped by a peeling icon gaudy as a circus bill and exactly three times as tall as the shack. The icon featured a ravaged Jesus dragging the cross toward Golgotha. Several soldiers were whipping Our Savior, who, under a crown of thorns the size of a tractor tire, stumbled on, drenched in blood. A perpetual queue of people, mainly children and old women half in mourning, were filing in one side of the shack and out the other. One hundred heaps were parked along the road.

"For fifty Boliveras, you can get in line to see part of Jesus' genuine crown of thorns," Jimmy said.

"Really," I said, craning my neck to study the grisly icon. "But it's only a small part," Jimmy added, as Luis Manuel swerved past a woman with a shawl pulled over her head. "In Caracas, they got a whole one."

"Verrrrrga!!" Jimmy yelled as Luis Manuel wheeled his pickup toward the sprawling mob at Tascabana. I figured there were easily 2,000 people already there. Some had driven from as far away as Ciudad Bolivar. Others had punished their burros upwards of two days across torrid plains to shoot the tubes, or to drink, or both. The City Council and the National Guard had drummed up various safety procedures—all unheeded—and a phalanx of soldiers was there to enforce them.

From atop two junkers parked on opposite banks of an Olympic-pool-sized mudhole, the Mayor of Tascabana (Don Armando Brito, renowned for reading nothing except funny papers and the Bible) and one Coronel Baltazar Negretti de Negron megaphoned commands, which sounded like so much white noise, challenged as they were by the blaring stereos of five-hundred cars that girded the sump in a formation so tight that Luis Manuel, Jimmy and I had to tread over trunks, roofs and hoods to gain the tubes. At the waterline, entrepreneurs peddled deep-fried pig skin and bottled pop, and the lagoon was awash in trash equaling that of a World Cup soccer match. Enriched by the harshest liquors, hundreds laughed, jeered and shouted, anxious to go before their valor washed downstream. Bobbing pop cans, plastic wrappers, soccer balls, a guitar, two stray dogs and dozens of humans rapidly drained down the twenty-odd tubes, continuously replaced by roof hoppers on the rebound, bruised and horror-stricken, but ready for more. However, Luis Manuel seemed suspicious of the thick layer of foam in the water and would have nothing of this common man's launch.

"He wants to go to the higher pool," Jimmy moaned. "Faster tubes up there."

"Lead the way," I said. Jimmy looked like a convict marching to the gallows, yet seemed dead-set on getting hanged.

Our bare feet made rude slurping sounds in the mud as we followed Luis Manuel a quarter mile to the higher pool. This one had a tenth the people, half the tubes, and five times the soldiers. I waded in and stroked for a tube, but—Alto! A soldier would first have to take an "official" ride.

"Por que?!" begged Luis Manuel.

"El gordo, el gordisimo!" laughed a private, knee-deep in the murky water and clutching a rifle that pre-dated de Miranda's landing at Corto. It seemed some fatty had just taken off, so the scout would have to go first—to flush the tube.

Luis Manuel grabbed our arms and the three of us kicked over to another tube and slipped in—me clutching Luis Manuel's ankles, Jimmy, sheet-white and trembling, clinging onto mine. The turns were five-degree welded elbows, so at turn one, the three of us were jolted apart, as were half of Luis Manuel's remaining teeth and most of my vertebrae. Due to the constant water flow, the tubes were well mossed, and in seconds we were vaulting down into blackness. We slammed through another turn. "If I hit another bend, I'll dent the fucking tube," I thought, trying to ignore the screams of careening bodies. After a long minute and hundreds of yards, just as my stomach had shrunk to the size of a chickpea, light showed far ahead. We rifled out and free-fell into casual water, flailing to avoid hitting each other. We swam to shore and started rubbing our barked hips and shoulders. Nobody could stop laughing and Jimmy carried on as though he'd just slain the Hydra with his bare hands.

"It takes a set of bollas to take that ride, chico!" he yelled, "Bollas grandes!"

We kicked back in the mud, and watched for a while. I noticed that better than half of the tube-shooters were women and girls, but Jimmy kept on about his "bollas grandes."

The fifty-foot cement wall was festooned with more than forty pissing tubes, whose positions varied from below the waterline to near the top of the wall. From the profusion of tubes, I felt assured of Luis Manuel's claim that all pipes terminated here, and Jimmy breathed a little easier knowing some strange pipe would not spit him out in Paraguay. Screaming bodies came whistling forth, backward, upside down, landing on friends who had landed on friends. Everyone howled as the human bullets, stunned and dumbfounded, hobbled over to the bank, collapsed into the mud and licked their wounds.

"Cooooooono!" shrieked Luis Manuel.

I caught sight of a crazed youth who came rocketing out at the forty-foot level. His scream could have turned the stomach of a granite statue, and he pawed the air like an airborne cat as everyone below dove for their lives. WHOP! A ten-point belly flop. Yet he quickly stroked to the bank and raced off.

"Vamo, pue!" Luis Manuel said, jumping up.

"The bastard can't let that kid out do us," Jimmy said to me, white and shaking again.

We scampered after the kid, but lost him in the crowd. Plodding on after Luis Manuel, I noticed steady traffic staggering to and from a cordoned area surrounded by a dozen menacing soldiers.

"Oh, that?" Jimmy said, relieved that we'd lost the kid. "Liquor is strictly forbidden anywhere near the tubes. Too dangerous. But anyone willing to walk to that huddle can drink himself half dead and go right back to the pipes. You figure it out."

Back at the high mudhole, Luis Manuel spotted some footprints leading off, and the three of us tracked them half a mile to a green puddle, vacant save for the kid we'd just seen delivered forty-feet above the aqueduct. Luis Manuel beamed as the kid peered into five half-submerged tubes.

"These babies look a little rusty," I said.

Luis Manuel scoffed, and with a casual flick of the hand said most of the pipes were old to begin with, and it didn't matter anyhow because all pipes led to Romo.

Luis Manuel questioned the Indian, who answered by slipping headfirst into the middle pipe.

"Oh, sheeeet." Jimmy said, as Luis Manuel waded over to the middle tube. "We better...take this one...feet first, chico. Better to have your feet take those bends than...your goddamn cabeza."

Sage advice, since shortly after entering, the tube angled down sharply, slammed round a bend and shot us into the darkness at speed. I blindly tried to stay centered on the slime, clutching my gonads, praying I'd find no U-turns or sloppy welds. The kid's screams died off. Then, suddenly, the pipe vanished beneath me, and I tumbled through the darkness ten feet, twenty, God only knows how far to splash into some sort of tank. No sound from the kid. I thrashed for Jimmy and we clasped hands, treading and terrified, only to be whisked into a whirling eye like that in a draining bathtub. We gasped what we reckoned were last breaths as the vortex sucked us down a thin, vertical shaft. In two seconds—which lasted a century—we smacked bottom and were gushed out into a larger pipe, known so only by the more gentle curvature beneath our accelerating gams. Then we pitched down a ramp so steep our arms flew up, and we started racing all over again, only slightly reassured by the stale air and Luis Manuel's distant screams. His shrieks shortly gave way to something that sounded like a drumstick raked across a mile-long charrasca, a stuttering, wrenching sound we soon matched when we ground across a corrugated stretch that tweaked and pummeled every joint. We slammed into an elbow that knocked me so hard I saw stars despite the total darkness.

The aqueduct was way behind us now, and in total silence we whistled along for several straight miles, regaining some wits, and a numbing terror. Finally, I managed a scream, as did Jimmy, somewhere behind, and finally Luis Manuel and the kid, both well ahead. We were helpless but to course through the darkness. Then, we bruised off a final bend and shot for a pinhole of light. I breathed again, bashed across a final washboard and only half realized my fifteen-foot freefall into more mud than water.

No one could tell how long our ordeal had taken, only that the mud had dried before anyone could rise. I wobbled toward moving water to soak and check for injuries. The kid had a strained neck and didn't know if he was dead or in Patagonia. Luis Manuel rubbed his collarbone and blood trickled from a gash on his chin. Jimmy hobbled around in circles, mumbling about slaying the Cretan Bull, breaking the Diomede Steed, branding the Cattle of Geryon, plus a load of gibberish no one understood. The distant sound of truck horns proclaimed the autopista several miles away. Not a great distance, but we'd be hoofing it naked since the tubes had stripped the trunks off all four of us.

Candles for Ulak

We'd beaten Father Ian Gordon to Ijende by one month. My partner, Dean, had gotten Father Ian drunk a few times and was always borrowing condiments or novels from him, but they were very different men. Father Ian and I were pretty thick, though. A gray but vibrant Benedictine, he never pressed me on the Catholic bit, and I respected him for toughing it out in Ijende. I also thought he was crazy. Few natives would even look at him. The last priest had escaped the valley only because he'd had a .12 gauge scatter gun and a waiting plane. The government had recently made their presence felt to the extent that occasional outsiders were rarely bothered anymore, just ignored. Father Ian and I were outsiders, and got through many nights studying the local dialect, or "tok ples," and reading old military chronicles about Ijende.

When the Allies battled the Japanese for New Guinea during World War II, they set up Intel operations in the most outlying jungle. One camp went up in Ijende, but not without a fight. Local natives—the Kuku Kuku—cared little for each other, even less for outsiders who plowed up their gardens to install bunkers and Quonset huts. Dozens of GIs were killed by these natives while establishing the Ijende camp and scores of Kuku Kuku were machine-gunned in turn. The Allies built the airstrip, and later Australian colonists established an outpost but never managed to tame the bellicose tribesman. Then a Trappist priest from Brisbane arrived and within a decade he had every last warrior hailing Mary. Father Alfred Winston must have been a remarkable man, part saint, part sovereign. According to Father Ian, he established a slew of jungle shrines and a Catholic school in Ijende, with three reed-walled classrooms and six Carmelite sisters. For a dozen years, Ijende might have been the staunchest Catholic enclave on earth, outside the Vatican.

Then, four years ago, blackwater fever came into the valley and carried off Father Alfred Winston.

Six months after Father Alfred died, the Ijende school was empty and the Carmelite sisters gone. The church sent over a string of different clerics to succeed Father Alfred but none could; they all either quit the place, or were driven out if they'd tried to force things. Yet the Kuku Kuku still practiced their own version of Catholicism, and very faithfully.

Dean and I employed more than a dozen natives in our work—seismic blasting, probing the bedrock for oil. Every noon we'd break, and whether huddled in swampland or bush or balanced on living rock, the natives would stoke some incense and haul out a crucifix and a small brass statue of the Virgin. They would light several votive candles and pray their novenas and rosaries and what not. They all did this, all but Kari Dumba.

Born in Ijende, Kari Dumba was Kuku Kuku only in race. Raised in the Catholic school during Father Alfred's reign, he'd gone on to college in Melbourne and had returned to Ijende as a kiop, a sort of bush ranger. He knew all the bush pilots and would often fly out to Wau or Kerema and bring back liquor and magazines and other stuff we couldn't get in Ijende. On one of these runs, Kari Dumba left on a Beechcraft Twin. Three months passed and he still hadn't returned. I later learned he'd wangled a transfer to Wewak, on the north coast, 300 miles away. That amazed me because we'd always gotten along and his sneaking off left us in a bad way. None of the other native workers spoke English, and my pidgin was pretty ragged when things got technical. Dean, a raw, irreverent Tasmanian, hadn't learned a word of the native tongue.

About a month after Kari left, a great commotion and celebrating grew among the Kuku Kuku. They finally had their Queen, they said, a girl named Ulak from Kantoba, a mountain village two days march away. She was "mogatu," divine, the workers promised.

Dean and I continued with our seismic tests, working with the same dozen natives. We noticed that the workers had replaced the brass Virgin with a wooden idol in their noon ritual. I asked the native foreman, Ufafakoos, about it, and he said, "Ulak." Ulak had replaced the Virgin Mary. In another month, Ulak totems had sprung up all over the valley. Dean and I had talked about slogging up to Kantoba to do some scouting—and to meet this Ulak as well—but we knew the whole area was limestone so thick we'd need an atomic bomb to do any seismic work up there, and besides, we were busy enough around Ijende. We didn't much care who the Kuku Kuku worshipped so long as it didn't interfere with our work. Shortly, it did.

The Kuku Kuku suddenly put down their tools and refused to pick them back up no matter how much shag tobacco or unblended Scotch we offered. Their reasons were equivocal and varied from native to native, but it was all tied up with Ulak the Queen, and her fantastic visions and talk about redeemers. Ulak was pregnant and they were going to wait. They'd squat down and lean back on their heels, all bemused by the beauty of the thing, each mind hanging out in the future when the miracle should come down. The poor had become the creators.

There were only Kuku Kuku in the whole Ijende valley, so there was no other help to enlist. The government sent several ministers to Ijende, hoping to persuade the Kuku Kuku to resume helping us. They would not. Ulak was pregnant. They were going to wait. What they were waiting for and what it all meant was part genius, part guile, and was something I had trouble sorting through even after it happened. Whatever, the ministers gave up trying to make the natives return to their sledge hammers, and told me over the shortwave that in a week we would have a dozen army laborers, flown up from Port Moresby. Several days after the natives began their strike, Father Ian hobbled into our hut, seeking a favor. He had an abscess on his leg, slow to heal in the clammy bush, and he still couldn't walk without a cane.

Father Ian said he'd reported to his bishop about Ulak the Queen—the little he knew about her—and Bishop Clarence Roth had radioed in that he was personally coming to Ijende to settle things up. Father Ian wondered if Dean and I might guide the bishop to Ulak's home in Kantoba, a two-day march north. Since it would take several more days before the army laborers arrived from Port Moresby and we could start blasting again, we agreed to guide the bishop. If it weren't for the leg, Father Ian would have guided the bishop himself.

"What gives with this queen?" Dean asked. Father Ian must have anticipated this question because he pulled a copy of The Catholic Times from his pocket and handed it to Dean.

Holed up as he was in Ijende, I figured Father Ian knew less about Ulak than we did. Dean and I were with the natives nearly every day, ranging over the whole area. Yet owing to the natives' slippery talk, and the fact that we'd never seen her, we knew next to nothing about this queen. Father Ian had studied logs in the now-defunct Ijende Catholic school, however, and had learned the following: As an infant, Ulak had been found abandoned in the jungle and brought to the school. Her natural parents were never found, so the Carmelite sisters adopted her. In time, Ulak won the regard of all the sisters and even the sainted Father Alfred, who considered her something of a marvel. By age thirteen, she'd breezed through high school equivalency exams. Father Alfred's last day alive was spent with Ulak, then fourteen, who knelt alongside the priest's deathbed for seven hours. When Ulak emerged, Father Alfred was dead.

Dean finished browsing the magazine article and handed it to me. "A proper yarn," Dean said, "If you fancy that kind of thing. But how does Ulak figure into it?"

"I'm not quite sure," Father Ian said. "There's certain similarities between what's written here, and what Ulak has—or what the natives have said she...." He trailed off. "I just don't know."

I glanced over the article entitled, "Miracle in Medugorje." About sixteen months back, in the mountain village of Medugorje, Croatia a phantasm or spirit began appearing to six children. The spirit identified herself as the Blessed Virgin Mary, Mother of Peace, and continued to appear to the children, who related their revelations to the parishioners. The Vatican initially downplayed the visions, but over time they were considered bona fide. I'd skimmed the article, but the description of what the Slavic kids had seen, or claimed to have seen, stuck in my mind:

"On this account, all the children are in agreement. The Virgin Mother is of tall stature with light skin and penetrating blue eyes. They all agree she is the most beautiful woman they have ever seen. She wears a golden crucifix with four rubies set in the corners and a great blue sapphire in the middle. Her dress is either of various hues or it routinely changes colors, and judging from the children's testimonies, the latter seems most likely. Curiously, none of the children have ever seen the Virgin's feet, which are forever shrouded in a cloud, or in some form of mist."

◆ ◆ ◆

Father Ian, Dean and I stood out on the little grass strip, staring into a bank of gray clouds. We couldn't see far, but could hear a bush plane about five miles away and nothing else but raindrops pocking the mud. The hot rain felt good on my bare chest but it couldn't wash away my edginess. Scores of natives always crowded the little strip whenever a plane landed, but this time it was vacant, not a single naked pickaninny or hunched old kanaka screaming at the metal bird. But I felt one hundred native eyes pressing on us from the hardwood trees. Father Ian had told one native that the bishop was coming. Now they all knew. Their hiding was a bad sign, for all of us.

The Cessna 240 punched through the clouds, lined up for the grass airstrip, landed hard and bounced all the way to the far end. The bishop jumped out, stalked over to us and curtly shook Father Ian's hand. Six foot-four and restless as a puff adder, there seemed more fullback than father in Bishop Clarence Roth. He barely nodded at Dean and me before charging off for our cluster of little huts, Father Ian hobbling behind him. The six-hour junket of jungle hops getting to Ijende had been hard on him, apparently.

We hadn't been inside ten minutes when the bishop began hammering on our door, ordering us to gather our stuff and get on with it.

"This mic's a live one," Dean said, calling to the bishop to hang on. "He might back us into a corner, if we let him."

Dean slipped a Berreta .38 into his rucksack and patted it. He carried the pistol with him every time we ventured into the jungle. He'd never once pulled it out of his sack, but always knew just where it was. So did I. Our unstated agreement was that if shooting ever came down, I would probably do it.

An afternoon thundershower pelted us as we hit the muddy trail toward the northern escarpment and Kantoba. He had to be fifty, but the bishop almost broke into a jog. I told him he might as well ease off because even if he sprinted the whole way we wouldn't get to Kantoba till late the next day. If anything, the bishop stepped it up, muttering about "the sheer impudence of it, this sacrilege." "That bugger needs to get laid," Dean mumbled. I just kept putting one foot in front of the other, trying not to worry about any of it.

We wound through the ancient shade, heading for Balbundi, our first stop along the route. The overhead brier closed snug as trellis mesh and the northern escarpment was lost from view. Just off the trail we passed a putrid boar carcass, teaming with a jacket of great red ants. We covered our mouths and marched on, away from Ijende.

With an hour of daylight left, the bishop, Dean and I stumbled across a dilapidated bush chapel. Crude to begin with, its bark walls were caved in, the reed ceiling sagged to the overgrown floor and the wooden crucifix, free-standing above the ridge pole, was barely discernible under a choking braid of vines. One hundred yards farther, we found Balbundi—not a village, just a dozen thatched huts. I knew that better than forty people lived there, but now the place was deserted. Not even the mangy, staring dogs. They had cleared out altogether. If they were simply hiding in the forest, no one could have kept the dogs from yelping. It was dead calm. They'd known we were coming.

"The bishop," I murmured. Even landslides couldn't drive the natives from their homes.

"What are you looking to do in Kantoba, anyhow?" Dean asked the bishop.

"Do?" the bishop replied. "Look what's happened since Father Alfred died. These people are Catholics. I'm the first bishop to ever come here and they all run off? The place has gone to the Devil, gone to that queen of theirs.

"And you plan to get it back," I said, remembering the reports I'd read about KuKu KuKu loosing arrows at GIs for walking through one of their sweet potato patches.

"You're afraid of these people, aren't you?" the bishop asked.

"I'm beginning to be afraid of you, or what you'll stir up," I answered.

"We've got to work here, don't forget," Dean added.

The Bishop regarded us for a moment. "So do I."

How far he was willing to push things, I did not know; but I suspected he was going to, and I very much doubted I wanted to be anywhere near him when he did. I suggested making for Warutapu, a village about an hour's hike away. I was curious to see if any natives were still there, but told the others that if we could gain Warutapu before nightfall, at least we might get something to eat. The bishop agreed.

Dusk had fallen when we staggered into the village. We wandered through the several dozen huts. Not a soul. Normally, natives were crammed into the huts like cordwood. Unless they had thrown together some secret village in the last week, which was preposterous, they were just bivouacked in the jungle somewhere. The cicadas were deafening, but nothing else stirred.

Shrieking rang out from one of the huts. Dean and I raced over to find the bishop inside the hut, facing a wizened old native woman too old to go with her people, wherever they'd gone. She wailed in dialect, holding out a wooden carving of Ulak in her hands.

The bishop heaved a breath and closed his eyes. He came back composed, and asked "What has this Ulak done?"

"It's not just Ulak," I said. "These people are only thirty years out of the Stone Age."

"This ain't Melbourne, Father," Dean put in.

The bishop glared at us, and scoffed.

"These people belong to God, not to the Devil, not to Ulak," he finally said.

"It's just daft superstitions," Dean said.

"Whatever it is, we can't just charge into Kantoba and have you steamroll this Queen."

"You'll see the machetes flash if you do," said Dean. "Believe it."

The bishop smiled smugly. "Ulak has taken the faith and bent it to fit her designs, and she's no right to do this. She makes Father Winston's death seem very cheap. And we are made cheap—everyone in this valley—if we laud her."

"We haven't even seen her," Dean said.

"Perhaps I'm wrong," the bishop said. "Perhaps Ulak is a miracle. I will listen to her. I will give my blessing or I will censure her. Tomorrow, just point the way and I'll go alone." The bishop turned back to the old native woman, who started shrieking again. Dean and I walked outside.

"Another hardhead," Dean said.

An ingrate, I thought. And he wasn't brave. The bishop could never go it alone. Unless you were fluent with the faint trails, the terrain would swallow you. Even Australian kiops took a compass into strange jungle. Sometimes they even dragged a line. Without one or the other, they would perish. For a moment I considered letting the bishop push on solo.

Dean turned toward the other huts. "I'm going to find some food."

I wandered back to a stream down by the trail to wash the mud off. I found a pool and waded in, wondering about natives fleeing their homes and an old woman waving a fetish in a bishop's face. None it this had anything to do with me, and I didn't want it to.

I'd had enough of hardheads, of the jungle, of all of it.

We'd been nine months marooned in the snarled and sweltering heart of no man's land—nine months of punishing rains, volcanic natives, tinned meat and sweet potatoes, no women, a little dysentery and a lot of seismic blasting. Our latest results looked promising, but both Peadmont Explorations and the Papua New Guinea government wanted more tests. And we both wanted out. So the business of trekking up to an outlying bush village to tell some native what to say or what not to say was starting to seem pretty weak.

The forest was black and my mind was made up when I waded out of the stream and threaded back to the village. I met Dean inside the biggest hut. He'd found a couple of pitch candles but no food.

"We're marching the bishop back to Ijende," I said. "This expedition's got trouble written all over it."

"You go back, then."

"What's this bishop mean to you, anyway?"

"Nothing. But I ran out of liquor and have fuck-all to do in Ijende."

The wailing had died off at the old woman's hut.

"I'm no bleeding adventurer, mate," Dean said. "But damn, how often you get a chance to meet some bush queen you'd think just shat in the Pope's miter? Now that's my kind of queen."

"I say we bag the whole thing—just leave her alone."

Dean chuckled for a bit and said, "The bloody white man can never leave anything alone. You know that." But the business was getting more reckless by the moment, and we both knew it. "If the bishop starts stirring the grief," Dean said.

"We drag him off," I cut in.

Dean nodded his head. "Immediately."

◆ ◆ ◆

We awoke at sunrise, starving, stiff and tired. The bishop stumbled from the old native's shack. His tenure on the island had given him native fluency in Niu Guini pidgin and he positively needed it to have placated that woman. When Dean asked him about it, he tossed out an off-hand reply suggesting his mastery at sorting out a crisis. The bishop repeated his offer to go on alone, and said nothing when he found out he didn't have to. We headed out on the three-hour uphill grind for Kantoba. The rains had stopped. The bishop had become a secondary concern to our empty stomachs.

We quickly entered the darkest region of triple-canopy jungle. Dornick outcrops, spangled with moss and fluted orange fungi, rose from the thinning verdure. Monkeys screeched high overhead as stray birds, distant and lonely, shot through the muted haze between trees. It was so humid our breath was like smoke. We plodded on.

In an hour, the terrain steepened. A tangle of lianas and rip-saw vines gave way to abrupt limestone slabs, the onset of the escarpment. The slabs soon converged at a ridge, the craggy path narrowing as we climbed up and out of the trees. We stopped many times, saying nothing, panting hard. Beyond, the path closed to about two feet wide, the land plunging away on both sides as the trail snaked up and into a fog bank. It leveled off on a small plateau at the roof of the world, surrounded by an iron-wood grove. Kantoba.

The village consisted of a dozen detached, stone terraces, each sustaining ten to thirty huts. On the central most elevated terrace stood a large circular thatched dwelling—and nothing else. Aside from two natives milling about this ultimate terrace, and a pack of panting dogs, Kantoba was vacant—better than 600 natives, gone.

We followed the bishop up to the high terrace and the two natives moved quickly over to us. Both were big, stone-faced and grave. Both wore thatches of Kunai grass in front and back, secured with a rattan belt. Their mouths were blood bins of betel nut spit, their few teeth stained black as shards of obsidian. Under a smearing of ash and putrid pig fat gleamed chestfuls of crude tattoos. Like most bushmen, each clutched a long machete in his right hand; they had a red history of knowing how to use them.

The bishop asked about Ulak and the younger of the two natives thrust his chin toward the circular hut; but when the bishop stepped that way both natives grabbed his arms, insisting in brusque pidgin that Ulak couldn't be disturbed just then. They exchanged some edgy words and I thought for a moment that the bishop might try to fight his way to the hut. I'd wager it was the first time anyone had denied him anything. Wisely, he shook the natives off and leaned back against a small boulder. Atop the boulder rested a crucifix and a small carving. Ulak. The bishop stared up at this and when he turned back to me, his face was hard as stone.

A Kuku Kuku elder emerged from the circular hut. I knew this man, Timbunke, and feared him. He'd badgered the natives who worked for us and had clubbed the hell out of one man who had challenged him. Dean hated Timbunke and there had nearly been a fight between them over the clubbing. Timbunke clutched an ironwood spear with a jagged quartz tip lashed to the end, and with it, motioned us to follow him back inside. Why he was letting us inside in the first place I couldn't then figure out, and I let him know with a glance that I didn't like any of it. We had to duck to get through the low entrance.

The hut buzzed with flies and reeked from smoke and dark puddles of betel nut spit. The principal light seeped in through the small entry, so it took a minute before my eyes adjusted to the dim surroundings and I could make out Timbunke and several other natives slinked against the back wall. Timbunke signaled us to sit down, facing Ulak. That put the elders' backs flush against the reeds, with the our backs to them, so I reckoned they had things just as they wanted.

Ulak sat on a rattan mat, her legs crossed. Aside from a short reed skirt and a brass crucifix around her neck, she was naked. She couldn't have been more than nineteen, twenty at the most. Full breasts and a distended stomach said she was very much pregnant. She bore none of the blank wonder seen on many native faces and her black eyes were quick, savvy and luminous. Maybe it was these eyes or the agreement of her features that set her off like that, but I couldn't take my eyes off her. Nobody could. She didn't move, glowing in the cluster of half a dozen pitch candles that burned around her.

She resumed talking to the other natives. Not in pidgin, but in dialect, so neither the bishop or I could understand a word. But her poise and command were apparent and superb, mainly because she made no effort to affect them. After a few minutes she closed her eyes and I studied her closely. Aside from a presence that would shine in any crowd, life seemed to move around Ulak in a way I couldn't explain—as though more of her was present in that hut, in that moment. When she opened her eyes, they penetrated the bishop.

"Nem bilong yupela Ulak?" the bishop began.

She smiled wryly and in a thick Australian accent said, "We'll talk in English. Pidgin is too limited."

"Your English is excellent, Ulak."

"I was raised by the Carmelite sisters, who rarely let me out of their sight for fourteen years," she replied bluntly.

"Do you know who I am, Ulak?"

"I don't know your name, but I knew you were coming before you did."

"What's that supposed to mean?"

She canted her head forward and said, "The Blessed Virgin warned me about you."

Such an outlandish piece of hokum would have sounded absurd coming from anybody else but Ulak had gravity enough to pull it off. Or maybe it was that behind it all I couldn't sense the presence of an ego as I normally understood it. She was sitting right there, yet seemed remote as the Crab Nebula.

"How can you speak for the Blessed Virgin?"

"I speak only for myself."

The bishop nodded severely and asked, "How do you know it's the Virgin who speaks to you?"

"Are you saying the Virgin has never spoken to anyone?"

"You haven't answered my question."

"It's vain of you to think that I must. A pious man would only be interested in learning the Virgin's message."

"Why does the Virgin counsel you?"

"I have a great work to do."

"You are divine, then?"

"To anyone who honors Our Savior."

To that point, the bishop couldn't have looked more smug in a gilded see; but beads of sweat now welled on his forehead. Maybe some part of him wanted to believe the Virgin would talk directly to a mortal. It supposedly had happened before. But if I'd learned anything from hiking the bishop up there it was that he wasn't concerned with Virgins at all, rather power. This was a turf war, plain as water. I didn't know what angle Ulak was working—not all of it, anyway—but I quietly marveled to see this orphaned bush kanaka, or whatever she was, challenging the bishop at his own game.

"How does the Blessed Virgin appear to you?" the bishop asked.

Ulak looked uncertain, as though she hadn't heard him.

"What does She look like?" he repeated. Ulak still said nothing and the bishop finally said, "Is the Blessed Virgin naked, Ulak?" "Do you think God is so poor he can't afford clothes for his Daughter?" she said.

The bishop smiled at her bare torso. "You tell me." He'd found his angle, and had regained his imperial command.

Ulak shook her head. "It is no use, Father. What will happen was determined nearly 2,000 years ago."

"It's all a delusion," the bishop said, "And I've come to expose it. And by the power of God, I will."

But nothing the bishop said had the slightest effect on her composure. Ulak fixed her gaze on the bishop and said, "The Virgin is tall, her skin is fair and her eyes are blue as the sky. She's very beautiful. She wears a large gold cross around her neck. The cross has red stones in each corner and a big blue stone in the middle. She wears a dress that always changes color."

The bishop remained silent for several beats. When he opened his mouth, I had to strain to hear his voice.

"And her feet?"

"Her feet?"

"Yes, what do her feet look like?"

"Nobody sees the Virgin's feet," she said assuredly. "They're always covered in fog."

From the second he'd charged off that Cessna two days before, he'd never once considered Ulak anyting but a perfect swindle, and had gambled everything on her heavenly description being counter to the orthodox rendering. When she pulled out her hole card with the fog bit, the bishop had lost, and he knew it. Now he was left to fathom the apotheosis of a topless femme fatale in a village of neo-savages who considered grubs a delicacy and bartered with their first born—and the notion froze him still as a granite santo.

Several times Ulak glanced at me. I'd done everything but wink at her. When again her eyes flashed on me they were those of a gambler betting more than she could cover, and I was starting to get a feel for the thing.

"When did the Holy Mother start—start counseling you?" the bishop stammered out.

"You can only understand so much at one time," Ulak said.

I knew that for a teenaged pregnant bush kanaka to tell an eminent bishop that he didn't have the spiritual acumen to fathom the Second Coming was a tactical error; but the clencher was that, so far as he could tell, the very mandate that he'd gone there with had, through divine providence, been snatched from his hands and given to a native. Their roles now reversed, Bishop Clarence Roth got his first taste of subjugation, was enraged by the naked fact of it, was confounded that it could possibly happen. Whether he could not, or would not except it was extraneous, for it all amounted to the same thing—trouble.

"Why has the Most Precious Virgin—" the bishop grumbled, struggling to his feet. "Why has She—"

As he groped for words, the elders sprang up. The air was charged, and wanted clearing before the roof blew off for the enormity of the blasphemous contradictions confronting the bishop. I grabbed the bishop's arm and dragged him outside. Dean followed. We all needed air and the bishop had to steady up and, if not accept the face of things, at least let the whole business play out till this sorcery, like all sorcery, came to dust and ashes in the end. The bishop staggered away and slouched back against the boulder. If wrath and confusion were solid matter, his could have damed the Torres Straight at high tide.

Dean came over to me, lit a cigarette and drew furiously on it. "You read that magazine, and Ulak's description was to the frigging letter what those Yugo—"

"It's not what you think," I said.

Dean toed the butt into the mud. "Ulak came to this dump before that all started with those Slavs." I nodded. "I think there's something to it," Dean said. "Hell, I don't know. It's awful strange, though."

"It's not what it looks like, Dean."

"You don't know that—not for a fact you don't."

"The girl's just playing out her hand. I don't know where she got it—"

"Okay, it's smoke and mirrors all the way," Dean cut in, "And I never bought that Virgin yarn anyway but that girl's a piece of work, mate. Seeing her carrying on—it's weird, that."

Whatever it was, the sanctioned, sacred and very white bishop would never let things lie. Yet there was no reversing any of it now. I lingered over those quick little glances from Ulak. During all her years in that blighted village God alone knew what had happened to her, or cared.

The bishop stared out over the valley below, his lips moving slightly, as if he was praying at the steps of some abstract monolith. He'd been hopping between Australia and New Guinea for fifteen years and believed he'd seen humanity with all the varnish off it, raw and furious. In fact, he knew almost nothing about the island, less of the people who lived there. Shortly, Timbunke motioned us back in. Ulak went right into it.

"As it's written in Scripture, our Lord will return. And here, in Kantoba."

"In Kantoba?" said the bishop.

"And very soon. A few weeks, only."

Candlelight played across the bishop's face and the hard shadows heightened the grotesqueness of the scene.

"Do you believe in the prophesies, Father?"

"I believe—in the biblical prophets."

"But a poor bush kanaka could not possibly know these things, could she? Isn't that what you are thinking, that it's a great sacrilege, what I'm saying?" Her voice had no edge or malice in it.

"I've said nothing to—"

"—But I'm not of this world. I was begotten, not made. And I know what you think before you think it. You came to refute me and Our Savior. But the Virgin told me you were coming, so I was prepared." Her black eyes needled him. "You are my Judas, Father."

"Judas?" the bishop spat out.

"Judas incarnate, and you don't even—"

"I've devoted my whole life—"

"—I am the second Blessed Virgin. I've been chosen to bear Our Savior back into the world. As you, Father Judas, cannot."

The words were no sooner off Ulak's lips than her spell was shattered. The bishop jumped up—to refute Ulak, his own life, God, everything in heaven and earth for all I knew.

"Lies!" he screamed, his face the very color of rage. I leapt to my feet and grabbed the bishop just as he lunged for Ulak. He struggled ferociously. I heard the natives stir behind him as I got a foot planted, and swung the bishop around. It all seemed to happen in time lapse. I only remembered a charging native—Timbunke—and a hot pain in my side. Then a gunshot.

I dropped the bishop and grabbed my side. Timbunke had run his spear clean through Bishop Clarence Roth and had grazed me as well. Dean had shot a round through the reed ceiling, and held the Berretta over his head, his hand shaking uncontrollably. I snatched the pistol, sprang over to Ulak and flushed the pistol to her temple. The natives froze, still holding their spears. Wheezing hard in his last throes, the bishop clawed around to face Ulak, one hand on the fixed spear, his other hand stretched toward Ulak. Even as the breath died in his mouth he wanted to pull her down. He slumped and lay still.

"Don't move," I yelled at Ulak, "Don't move at all." I quickly glanced around. I didn't know what I would do if anyone tried me, but Timbunke was going to get the worst of it, and I let him know with my eyes. Nobody moved because they knew me, knew I was satisfied to be just like they were.

"How's the bishop?," I finally asked Dean. It was obvious, but Dean checked his pulse anyway.

"Dead."

I glared at Timbunke as Ulak fidgeted. The bishop was dead, and though nobody but me knew it, so was all hope for the queen. Word would spread, the army would charge in, throw Ulak into chains, beat a confession out of her till the big men nodded, then chuck her and child back into the mud, fallen angels.

"We're walking out of here," I finally said. Ulak didn't move or say a word. "And you're staying here. All of you."

"We were prepared for this. It was meant to happen."

"Tell them what I said."

"It was always meant for you to take the heretic away."

"Tell them anyway."

She did, and the natives slowly lowered their spears.

"You okay?" Dean asked.

"Yeah," I lied, wobbling. I took a bloody hand from my side but kept the gun trained on Ulak and my eyes on the elders. "Better get that spear out," I muttered.

Dean yanked on it, but it had gone through the dead man completely and was hung up. He yanked again and it still would not come out. That an itinerant, grifting seismic engineer from Tasmania could even end up in that smokey lair had him fumbling. A dead bishop Iscariot and a coal black Mother of God made him almost useless. "Bloody hell."

"Try again," I raged.

Dean said nothing, just blocked his foot off the bishop's chest and heaved. The spear finally came free. I moved slowly away from Ulak.

"Nobody leaves this hut," I started.

"The threat has passed," she said. But this time her voice betrayed her. Heaven's anointed perhaps, but she wasn't the Mother of God yet, just a rattled young woman with a dead bishop at her feet. I knew she was glad to stay behind. It was written all over her ashen, bloodless face.

Dean and I dragged the bishop outside. Nobody followed. Nobody needed to. The sun was slipping off the horizon as the natives streamed out of the surrounding grove. In an instant, every native from every abandoned village crowded the trail, hundreds of them, each holding a little bush candle—a dollop of pitch inside a bamboo plug—1,000 flames flickering in the dusk. I knew it was all part of a grim plan, and if things turned against the Queen, we would have to answer to a mob.

We shouldered the bishop's body and stumbled down the stone path, the natives chanting, "Oo lau, moge, Oo lam Ulak."

They parted as we filed through them, chanting, staring, old men and children, each with a candle, all waiting for the heretic to leave and the Messiah to return. Nobody moved. "Oo lau, moge, Ol lam Ulak" droned on like a bleak dirge. It was dark when we gained the lower trees, and we both knew the worst part of the work lay ahead.

The bishop was very heavy and the night very black, but we knew the trail well so we pushed on. "It's gotta be bullshit," Dean kept repeating. But he didn't sound so sure about it. He was a staunch atheist, but an even stauncher gambler, and so was very superstitious and didn't know what to believe. "It's gotta be bloody bullshit." I put one foot in front of the other and tried to block it all out. But my side ached and Ulak's face went ahead of me.

By the time we wobbled back into Ijende the next afternoon, we'd been going for twenty-three hours, hadn't eaten in forty, and the bishop's body was stiff as a plank of ironwood.

◆ ◆ ◆

Dressing my own wound, I gave a quick breakdown to Father Ian, hating it and hating myself. Father Ian listened stoically, maybe because among Catholics, a martyr is a hero. I took the blame but Father Ian quickly reminded me it had been the bishop's idea to go, and he would have gone alone—and gladly.

"I could have forced him back at Balbundi, and I should have."

"No, son," Father Ian said, "You're not his master, and he'd never want your grief."

"I'm not grieving for that hardhead," I said, glaring at the bishop's body, moldering in the heat. "He doesn't have to live with it. He's dead. It's Ulak. We just couldn't leave her alone, could we? We had to march in there and tell her that God doesn't talk directly to natives in thatched huts. A couple white kids see the same spook and magazines are published about it. But some bush queen? No. We've got to stick her face back in the mud."

"There are certain lies, monstrous lies, that are worth trying to stop," the father said mildly.

"It's all a lie. But it's our lie, isn't it? That makes it hallowed and just and funded. But when Ulak lies, it's monstrous." Father Ian stared at the ground.

Dean radioed Port Moresby. The Prime Minister quickly had the news, and sent the country's one Sikorsky helicopter and twenty-five troops directly to Ijende. To a struggling country heavily dependent on foreign aid, a bishop's murder would prove a P.R. disaster unless the government could quickly sort out their own version of events.

While they waited for the chopper, Dean broke it all the way down for Father Ian, even Ulak's description of the Virgin, and asked him what he made of it.

"She is said to be very—intelligent," said the father.

"She's at least that," Dean assured him. Then Dean explained the Father Judas bit, and all the rest. Father Ian couldn't respond.

"What's the chance this Ulak got hold of that magazine you showed us, or one like it?" Dean asked.

"None, I'm afraid," he muttered. "I just got it myself."

"But you knew about it, yes? Maybe Ulak learned about it as well."

"From whom?" Father Ian asked. "The Medugorje visions started long after the last priest driven off. And it's not the kind of theology I'd ever mention to the few natives who will listen to me here." It all seemed as unknowable as the grave and Father Ian looked about one foot into one. "I'm afraid there's only one explanation for the time being."

"Only one," I said. "The girl's stumbling around, pregnant in a potato patch, and she dreams up a way to get out of it. Who knows where she heard about that Slavic tale, but she did."

"How do you know that?" Dean asked. "You don't know any more about it than I do." Dean pulled on his cigarette.

"She couldn't help knowing her power and using it," I said. "That's all it is."

Dean wanted to argue but the long march and the stress and hunger and confusion all came to a head and he had started to laugh at the strangeness of the thing. But the laugh stuck in his throat. Father Ian expected to find out something and would remain in Ijende until he did. The copter and the troops arrived in three hours. I went down to the river to get away from it all.

◆ ◆ ◆

In Port Moresby, the inquiry started the next day and included high-level cabinet members, army colonels and a Catholic delegation led by a Cardinal flown in from Sydney, Australia. Arguments about native sovereignty and myths and heretics who had to be stopped went on and on. People shuttled back and forth between Port Moresby and Ijende for a week, but all they ended up with was one dead bishop and a mystery. The authorities tried to kill the story, but the news leaked out—minus the Virgin-Ulak-Second-Coming part.

Army troops had charged straight into Kantoba but Ulak had fled to parts unknown and the natives were not talking, they were just waiting for the Messiah to return. Twenty soldiers were waiting as well. A dozen were stationed in Ijende and clashing hourly with the natives there. Several of the soldiers had been wounded by spears and arrows and three clansmen had been shot. After a week, they still hadn't found Ulak and there was no word of any savior. Father Ian had nothing new to go on and the waiting game aged him by the hour.

Dean and I spent the week analyzing seismic results, sending daily transmissions to the lab in Cairns, Australia, and Peadmont Explorations decided to do some preliminary drilling in Ijende. Despite the detailed topographical maps we'd drawn, Peadmont asked us to assist the drilling team, to nail down the locations. We'd been mired in Ijende for an age, and the Peadmont brass had to promise us a thirty days paid vacation to stay on.

"Maybe a black Jesus will come strolling down the river before we bugger off," Dean said, pouring out a tumbler of Old Smuggler Scotch.

For two days, Dean and I went about our work with the drilling team, nailing down the sites, driving demarcation stakes and spray-painting day-glo arrows on the rock. The first site was in the southern valley, but the second day we slogged north to a village called Karoka, and the kanakas streamed out of their hovels to haze us. We had an attachment of ten armed soldiers, so the taunting meant nothing; but the bad things burning in every native eye said plenty.

Late that second night, Kari Dumba staggered into our hut. We hadn't seen him in ninety-five days and I still thought he was in Wewak, on the north coast.

"Fuck off!" Dean yelled the second he'd made out Kari's profile in the darkness. But Kari had a gash on his arm and a lump the size of an egg over one eye, so we let him in. He'd just hiked back from Kantoba.

"Give me a drink," he said. His legs were mud-caked, his clothes soaked and torn and he hadn't slept in three days. Dean poured him a drink, and he tossed it off straightaway.

"Give me another drink," he said.

"I don't think you need another drink," I told him.

"The hell I don't."

Dean handed him the bottle and he chugged it till Dean ripped it from his hands and said, "Jesus, Kari!" He was down to two bottles.

"Yeah, Jesus, "Kari moaned. "But he's not coming back, not to Kantoba he isn't."

"Sit down," I said. He did, and we waited.

"It's out of hand, it's gotten totally out of hand and it's my fault, goddamit to hell it's my fault." Kari shook his head and yanked at his hair. "She didn't have a choice, she had nowhere to turn. And neither do I, but I can't let it go on."

"Ulak," I said.

"Blame me. You can't blame her. They'd have stoned her if they'd found out. I should have never left, goddamit."

"Ulak," I repeated.

"Yeah. Ulak. She was my girl. She is my girl."

"You knocked her up and you bolted for Wewak."

Kari just sat there, swollen and limp.

"Isn't that what you did, Kari?" I said.

Kari slouched back against the wall. In five minutes, we had it all.

The Carmelite sisters could hardly have carted Ulak off to Australia after the Catholic school disbanded in Ijende; but she still felt abandoned nonetheless, for she had no place to go but Kantoba, where she squeaked by tending kids and slaving in sweet potato gardens. Kari had known Ulak since they were kids at the school. When he became a kiop and returned to Ijende, he'd often trudge up to Kantoba to visit her. In many ways, the only thing they had in common with the Kuku Kuku was each other. Ulak had an impossible time adjusting to native life, and every time Kari would fly out to Wau or Kerema, he'd bring back books and magazines for her, including religious journals filched from the bush parishes. One such journal described the miracle in Medugorje. Then Ulak got pregnant, and Kari bolted, and she faced impossible times in Kantoba, for an unwed mother is an outcast and the child a pariah. So she dreamed up a scheme that would transmute her from a pregnant orphan who had nothing to the Mother of God, who had it all. The natives bought it and priests and bishops and most of the rest of us were wondering as well. Shame had forced Kari back to Ijende, where he heard the miraculous yarn about this Queen Ulak. He'd dashed to Kantoba but no one would tell him where the Queen was. He'd fought with both the natives and the soldiers and he stumbled out of the village worse off than he went in, and now he couldn't keep it buried any longer. Dean gave him the bottle back.

"You'd better tell Father Ian about this," I said. Kari winced. The next day Dean and I joined the drillers on the river a half mile west of Ijende. When we plowed back to camp that night, Kari Dumba and Father Ian were waiting for us. The following morning, they were marching to Kantoba and Kari Dumba was going to tell the natives the truth. They wanted me along.

"Bad idea," I said. "Better wait and deal with Ulak alone or you'll have trouble." If the natives had murdered a bishop, they'd have a fine time with someone who'd buffaloed them, I reasoned. And I had no business up there, and would probably have to blow Timbunke's brains out if I showed back up there and ever hoped to leave. I went to the river and bathed.

◆ ◆ ◆

Father Ian, Kari Dumba, Dean and I spent all evening trying to devise some strategy, but every plan except wait-and-see had too much risk. Then late that night a soldier, wasted from a marathon jog from Kantoba, stumbled into the military tent in Ijende. Seconds later, Captain Julius Sumari, a stout Motu man in charge of the soldiers, rushed into our hut.

There'd been a riot in Kantoba, a bad one, that morning. The Captain didn't know the numbers, but several natives and soldiers were dead. The remaining troops in Kantoba were fleeing for Ijende. They had Ulak with them. She was injured but the runner didn't know how badly. The captain rallied his remaining soldiers while Dean and I got headlamps and daypacks and we all hit the trail around midnight. About dawn, and just past Balbundi, we ran into the other soldiers.

Most of them were in rough shape. They'd had to leave five dead in Kantoba, and felt lucky to get out themselves. One soldier, who couldn't have been over eighteen, had a hatchet wound to the trachea and could only breathe by grabbing his throat. Another soldier had an arrow deep in his lower back and another one clean through his shoulder and he wouldn't let anyone touch them. His drawn pistol kept anyone from trying. One had a shattered elbow with bone showing and three others had deep bloody wounds from "bik pella stones"—from being stoned. A medic had come along with us, but he was almost worthless.

I knew a little about first aid, did what I could for the wounded, then Captain Wingtee sent the fittest soldier off at a run to summon the country's one medi-vac. The other soldiers straggled on behind.

Shortly, another three soldiers stumbled along. They looked weary but unscathed, and they carried a makeshift litter fashioned from saplings, two coats and several belts. Ulak lay on the litter. It was hard to believe that the bloody and battered woman could ever have been Queen of the Kuku Kuku. Her face was pulp, both eyes swollen shut. No longer pregnant, her torso was rippled with raw welts. They'd made a thorough job of stoning her. She was just conscious enough to mumble to Kari Dumba, who was clenching Ulak's hand and choking and stamping his feet.

I checked her vital signs. "She's got some bad internal injuries," I said to Captain Sumari. "Get her to the medi-vac soon enough and she's got a chance—a slim one."

"Where's the baby?" Dean asked one of the soldiers. Captain Sumari translated the question into pidgin, and one of the soldiers motioned to the trail behind him. Another soldier was bringing it along, he said bitterly. It was alive, but men had died over it. He spit into the mud and stumbled on for Ijende.

"Christ, those kanakas changed their tune fast enough," Dean said.

Ten minutes later, the last soldier came down the trail. He cradled a coat and we heard the crying. He laid the coat down and there she was, a flawless newborn girl, wailing her tonsils out.

By the time we made it back to Ijende that afternoon, better than eighty soldiers and government people had choppered in to help unravel the story. It rained most of the day and the newly-erected tent city was a quagmire. Then the mess tent caught fire and things got worse from there. The only official news was that the man with the throat injury was recovering and Ulak was in the military hospital at Lae.

Late that night, Captain Sumari came into our hut. He wasn't as drunk as Dean, but recent events hadn't improved his uniform or his humor. He'd just gotten off the radio and, staring ahead, he told us how Ulak had gone into a coma that afternoon and had died of renal failure. "Too many stones," he mumbled. Kari Dumba had left with the medi-vac and was heading back to work in Wewak. He couldn't possibly tend a baby. So he'd left her with the Sisters at the Santa Rosinda convent in Port Moresby for the time being.

Red Rock

(from Mental Painting)

T he Del Rio rodeo didn't have roping or steer wrestling or any of that. It was a bull-riding competition, period. The sponsor saw that all the best cowboys were there (a $37,200 purse), and that the foremost stock contractors trucked in their biggest, surliest animals. It was billed as the "Bull-Riding World Championships," an invention, since it wasn't even a sanctioned event. It was the most bad-ass bull-riding competition in the world, though. Every cowboy said so. Jim Sharp, Tuff Hedeman and Ty Murry were there, the best in the business. But we came to see Jimmy "Legs" Maldonado. Back then, Jimmy was the only Mexican-American on the pro rodeo circuit, and whenever a rodeo hit New Mexico or Texas—or wherever there were other Mexicans—they all turned out to see Jimmy ride. And Jimmy was good. He'd won fifth place at the world championships in Vegas the previous season, and that year at Del Rio, I think he was third in earnings, and the season was young.

Most of the crowd had spent the day just over the border, in Acuna, and many of them were pretty oiled. When the stadium lights clicked on the sun still hadn't set and it was hot as hell and dusty. A water truck rolled through the arena and dampened the dirt and, at the crowd's request, turned the hoses on the stands. Then the announcer—who went by the name Ferris Honeyquim— sashayed around the arena with a wireless microphone, and over a John Philip Sousa march blaring on the P.A., in a hayseed drawl so thick I could scarcely understand him, gave a short speech about "these great U-nited States." Clutching a gigantic American flag on a ten-foot pole, Miss Del Rio—a shocking blond in a stars-and-stripes bikini she could have crammed in a peanut shell—cantered into the arena on a twelve-hand palomino, and all the drunks leaped up whistling and punching the air. As Miss Del Rio circled, the national anthem came over the P.A., and everybody took off their hats and held them over their hearts and sang, "Oh say can you see..." Then Ferris Honeyquim slid into a prayer so righteous and high-blown that John Calvin snapped up in his grave.

I glanced behind the corrals, where the cowboys had been limbering up and rosining their gear, and every one of them was down on one knee with their hats off, their eyes closed and their faces set serious as the day of judgment as Ferris Honeyquim beseeched "Our Lord Jesus Christ...." It seemed a bit much, but after five minutes, I knew otherwise.

The second Honeyquim said "Ah Men," a heavy-metal rock track exploded over the P.A. Honeyquim yelled, "Let's get ready to rodeo!" and the crowd exploded.

Dad had gone to college with one of the stock contractors, so we didn't have to sit in the bleachers, but got to stand on a scaffolding a couple of feet above the chute were the bulls are herded along, mounted and released through the gate into the arena. Behind the arena was a series of corrals, and according to the draw—which determined who rode what animal—particular bulls were prodded from the corrals and into a long, partitioned chute against the back wall of the arena. Dad and I walked along the scaffolding until we were just above the last partition, where we could peer straight down at the first cowboy, who nervously straddled the fence poles beside the first bull. The stall was just big enough for the bull, which snorted and rocked about as the cowboy eased onto his bare back. Several men cinched a rope around the bull just behind the big hump on its neck. On top of this rope was a thong handle for the cowboy's hand, around which the tail of the rope was lashed as tight as the cowboy could stand it. Then they cinched a second, "bucking rope" around the bull's belly, perilously close to its heroic pendulous balls—and they didn't merely cinch it; rather four men heaved till the rope was taut as the anchor chain on a battleship and the bull was so pissed off his colossal horned head kept rearing back to gore the cowboy. The bull jumped and squirmed and bashed the cowboy's legs against the sides of the stall, blind rage flashing from its red eyes, the stench of its savage breath mixing with steam welling off its body which wafted up and buckled my knees on the scaffolding. I had never seen bull riding before. But peering down into the chute at the ferocious animal and the crazy bastard strapping himself onto it, I felt I was looking into the gears of the American soul.

"...And Travis Pettibone is first up on Skoal Psycho!" Honeyquim yelled out in his Texas twang, and the crowd grew louder and the guy working the P.A. cranked up the rock track in competition. Travis Pettibone shoved his hat down with his free hand, gritted his teeth and nodded.

The gate flew open and two tons of snorting, bucking, chuck-roast from hell thundered out of the chute, spun one way, throwing its haunches so high it almost did a handstand, immediately snapping its huge, wrecking-ball head straight back. Travis was all flying limbs but somehow hung on and the crowd went off. Then Skoal Psycho spun the opposite way and yawed right into the fence, slamming Travis into a sheet metal sign for a pizza joint. The bull whirled away and Travis dropped limp to the ground, out cold. The clowns—"Bullfighters"—raced up and decoyed the bull toward a guy on a fleet black horse, who chased it toward an opened gate into the back corral. The bull shot through the breach knowing another guy was waiting back there to ease the rope off its gut.

The second the arena cleared, paramedics raced in with a gurney, loaded Travis up and wheeled him off. An ambulance had backed up to the rear of the arena, and had its rear door open. When they got the gurney there, Travis sat up and tried to get off, but a paramedic pushed him back down. They loaded Travis up, the ambulance raced off and another, lights flashing, backed up in its place. I ran back along the scaffolding to see the next rider.

Jimi Hendrix's "Astroman" blasted over the P.A. (No hayseed crooning here in Del Rio), and Honeyquim yelled "...And it's Cody Lambert on Cajun Moon." The crowd roared, the gate flew open, Cajun Moon shot out, stopped on a dime, snapped its haunches almost vertical and Cody Lambert torpedoed off into the night, landing in a heap. He must have wrenched something, but he desperately crabbed to his feet, then sprinted to the fence and clawed up it as the big brown Brahma bull rumbled after him. Cody was safe enough, clinging fifteen feet up the fence, but Cajun Moon kept snorting and bucking wildly beneath him, trying to loosen the rope that was virtually strangling its generous nuts. The frenzied crowd pelted him with oaths and beer bottles and cushions and anything not tied down. The clowns decoyed Cajun Moon around, and the man on the black horse drove him back into the corral.

"...And give a big Del Rio welcome to D.J. Mulroon, on 777!"

The gate flew open and a gigantic piebald bull vaulted out and hobby-horsed wildly just in front of the gate—hind legs, fore legs, hind legs, fore legs—but D.J. somehow hung on for four, five seconds and the crowd went crazy again. Then 777 juked a little to one side and D.J. got off center and slipped forward. The bull's rearing head slammed into D.J.'s chest and bashed him back to meet the monster's rearing flank, which slammed him right into the ground. It was a two-thousand pound one-two punch. The clowns raced up and got 777 away, but D.J. Mulroon didn't move, bleeding from his mouth and ears.

"That guy's dead!" I screamed to Dad, pulling on his arm.

The paramedics rushed in. After a few minutes, D.J. came around, but he wasn't going anywhere on his own. As Honeyquim compared the bull riders to astronauts and gladiators, interlarding his drift with quotes from Jeremiah and Winston Churchill, the paramedics fitted a cervical collar around D.J.'s neck, loaded him up on the gurney and to the applause of the crowd, D.J. waved a limp hand. Then they wheeled him off, loaded him up, the ambulance roared off and yet another one backed into the hot spot.

That was just the start of it. In the next fifteen minutes, I saw two more cowboys body-slammed to the ground, another pitched into the fence and knocked cold; I saw a cowboy from Arkansas get kicked in the groin, and another break his wrist after an electrifying cartwheel exit off a bull called Black Ratchet. Then came Buddy Dollarhide from Checotah, Oklahoma.

I think he was about the fifteenth rider out, and only the second to ride to the horn—eight seconds. But he couldn't get off clean. He landed with his legs crossed, and stumbling to get his feet under him, got stepped on. The clowns got the bull's attention and Buddy Dollarhide frantically limped off, but we could all see the jagged white bone jutting through a hole in his boot. They'd run out of ambulances, so Buddy Dollarhide had to slouch back on the stairs below the judge's booth and bear it, yelling "Goddamit! Goddamit to hell!" A couple other cowboys moved over to calm him, and an old man whose face looked like a saddle bag handed Buddy a short dog of Crown Royal. He took a long pull, winced, pulled up his pant leg and poured the rest straight into the top of his boot, screaming, "Son of a fucking bitch!!" as the amber liquor streamed out red through the hole in his boot and over the jutting white bone. He threw the bottle against a horse trailer. Finally another ambulance wheeled up and took Buddy away.

"Coming out with Waco's own Jethro Reeves on A-Bomb!"

My heart thumped and I couldn't get enough air. "How can they let this go on?" I yelled at Dad. I felt if the rodeo kept going, most of us would be dead within the hour, then the army would roll in and shoot the survivors for crimes against mankind. Only when I glanced down at the queue of cowboys limbering up on deck, their faces like stone masks, did I understand that all this had to exist. And we didn't create the idea anymore than Flavius or Nero did. The players had created it. They required it. Without it, they were just so many cowpokes with nothing but trampled Stetsons and their pride. What they met head-on down there in the arena was what it all comes down to in the end, the irreducible brute element. Jumping onto its back was a direct deed more real than water or air or even fire, and it snapped everyone fully awake.

After about three turns, A-Bomb threw Jethro onto his ass and a clown helped him stumble away to get his wind back.

"Come on, Carlos," Dad said, looking back, "Here he is."

We got right over the gate and there was Jimmy "Legs" Maldonado, easing onto a big tawny bull. He couldn't have been more than five-foot six, but was thick-necked, with arms like

Spartacus. He had brown skin, but there was no way he was all Mexican. Legs talked with that Texas twang you hear around Stevensville and Henrietta.

Legs slid forward so his rope hand was right at his crotch. Then he nodded quickly.

Anybody could see the way Legs rode—like Jim Sharp, Tuff Hedeman and even Ty Murry, even though he got bucked off—was different than the others. These guys were a little stronger, a little more confident, had a little better balance than the others, and always seemed to anticipate where the bull was heading and what he'd do. And they always stayed right over their rope hand, free hand cutting the air to steady them. When the horn sounded, Legs reached down with his free hand, loosened the lash, and using the bull's bucking action, let himself be flipped off, landing on his feet in a full sprint. All the Mexicans—including about fifty Mexican nationals who got day visas and had came over the border from Acuna—were sitting together on a bleacher off to the side, and they all cheered wildly. Legs had made it through the elimination round to the finals. His score wasn't huge, a seventy-three, I think, because his bull wasn't as testy as some of the others, so required less skill and moxie to stay on. But when a cowboy lasted till that horn sounded, and if he got away unscathed, the score seemed immaterial. That man had won, had beaten two-tons of whirling death, and no person living or dead would doubt it.

After about half an hour, the first round was over and there was a break while the judges figured out the next draw. Of the thirty-two riders, I think only nine had made it to the horn. Dad and I climbed down off the scaffolding and made our way over to the Mexicans.

It was a pretty wide mix of people we met in that crowd, from Humberto Juarez, a multi-zillionaire who owned Tecate Beer, to rustic vatos who had snuck in through a hole in the fence. In Mexico, men like Juarez wouldn't be caught at a funeral with most of the others, but in the arena they all kept together because they were Mexicans who had come to see Legs ride. I drank a Coke as the others drank beer, but couldn't join the conversation because Del Rio was my first rodeo, and I didn't know the riders or any rodeo argot. Then the draw was announced, and three-thousand grim "Ooooos" went through the crowd:

Ferris Honeyquim said Legs had drawn Red Rock. In the other bleachers, people were shaking their heads and shaking their hands in the air like they were on fire.

"Carajo!" cursed a man beside me.

"Red Rock! Verrrrrrga!" another put in.

"Who brought that bastard here?!" my dad asked.

"El Diablo, that's who," someone said.

"He'll kill our boy just like he killed Ike Rude," Humberto Juarez said. The man was genuinely mad. And scared.

"You think Legs will even try Red Rock?" someone else asked.

"Sheeeeet yes he'll try," Dad said in English.

Red Rock was a killer. Only three bulls in history had ever been more than five years on the circuit and never ridden to the horn. The other two, Oscar and Tornado, were both in the Rodeo Hall of Fame. In the past two years, Red Rock had killed three cowboys outright, and maimed a dozen others. Ronnie Seawall had a plate in his head courtesy of Red Rock, and felt he got off lucky. Most of the time, a cowboy came down with a sudden groin pull or bum elbow when he drew Red Rock. I don't think anybody had even tried to ride him in the last six months. But Dad was right. Legs Maldonado was going to ride Red Rock.

We made our way back onto the scaffolding, which now overflowed with photographers and a video crew from ESPN. The rock track kicked back in and when Honeyquim yelled, "Are we ready to rodeo?" the crowd went off again.

"Comin' out with Shoat Tremble on Doctor Gizmo!"

And we were up in midair again, all a blur of streaking limbs and kicking hooves. A crash and burn, a perfect ride to the horn, another rider smashed into the fence and the shrill wailing of the ambulance siren. But no stopping now, no turning back. It was like sitting on top of a rumbling volcano. Then, the ESPN video crew flicked on some lights, and the cameraman bent over the scaffolding and shot straight down, an assistant holding onto his waist. ZZ Tops' "She's got Legs" came over the P.A., and the volcano erupted.

"Yer dad-burned right ladies and gentleman," Honeyquim chimed in, "We're talkin' 'bout Legs Mallllllllldonado on that son of a biscuit Red Rock, orneriest bull this side of Hades. So grab the dog and hide the kids 'cause here comes Legs!"

"Let her rip!"

I heard the gate fly open, but the scaffolding was so crowded they didn't come into view until about three seconds into the ride. And Legs was still on board. Red Rock had bolted to near the center of the arena, and had gone into a flat spin. The animal was tawny brown streaked with black lines—like a gigantic, rippling chunk of baklava. He was no bigger than the other bulls, but his resolve to get Legs off was spectacular, his moves furious and unpredictable. After about five seconds, the crowd completely drowned out the music.

Then everything slowed to a crawl. Even the crowd sounded muffled and distant. Red Rock seemed to vault and spin and rear his horrible head in slow motion, long, scalding bolts of snot firing from his nose and freezing in mid-air. And Legs Maldonado seemed nailed to the back of the killer bull. Once, both his legs flew up over his head, then his body doubled over to one side so far that the bull's flank smacked his head and knocked his hat off. But Legs was still there, still over his rope hand, the great bull and the great cowboy melded together like a minotaur. Then the horn sounded and the world spun back up to speed.

But it wasn't over for Legs.

Red Rock broke into a wild, bucking sprint. And Legs' rope hand was hung up. He frantically tried loosing the lash with his free hand, clawing at the cinched rope between bounds, but it was no good. Three times they circled the arena, Legs flopping around like a rag doll, strapped in tight. Then, suddenly, Red Rock dug his hooves in and plowed to a stop: Legs flew over the horns as though shot from a cannon, somersaulting through the air and landing on his neck about thirty feet away, face down, limbs twisted about him. One of the clowns dashed up, and Red Rock turned and chased him twenty feet up the backstop fence (the arena doubled as a baseball park). He suddenly wheeled and rumbled after the other clown, who just managed to dive into a big red barrel before the crash of Red Rock's lowered head; and I swear to God that barrel sailed forty feet before hitting way the hell up the fence and thunking back to the dirt. The guy on the black horse dashed in. Seeing Red Rock charging right down the pike at it, the horse dug into a turn and bolted, sailed over the five-foot retaining wall at the far end of the arena and slammed broadside into the Pepsi-Cola stand. Red Rock pawed the dirt, shimmied, tossed his head in disdain and finally slipped through the open gate into the back corral.

Legs lay face-down and motionless, and the crowd was frozen. They cut the music. You could have heard a feather hit the ground. It seemed time and space had telescoped down to that little patch of dirt where Legs lay, dead still. Every person in that arena was thinking the same thing: If Legs were dead, if that cabron Red Rock had killed him after he'd ridden him to the horn, bull riding was all wrong, was a fiendish crime and Red Rock would have to be shot dead on aesthetic, if not moral, grounds.

Then, slowly, Legs drew himself up to hands and knees, and a low murmur ran through the crowd. The Mexicans swarmed from the bleacher and pressed up against the fence, crawling and climbing over each other to get a better look, but still saying nothing. The other fans were standing up and crowding the screen with eyes big as platters. Finally, the clown slithered from the barrel and, breaking from a daze, yelled, "Ge...ge...get up, Legs! You gotta get up, boy!" Painfully, excruciatingly, Legs wobbled to his feet, straightened, raised a fist tentatively over his head and moaned straight up into the night.

And all hell broke loose.

That little brown bastard had slain the Cretan Bull. People clamored up the screen and hung from the flimsiest purchase, screaming and rocking back and forth, nearly pulling the whole works down; and the Mexicans stampeded over the rails and into the arena; someone put a sombrero on Legs' head, and they started parading him around on shoulders to the strains of "She's Got Legs" cranked so loud people could have heard it in the Yucatan. Then, the other cowboys came into the arena and hoisted Legs up in the air as well.

After a while, Honeyquim managed to clear the arena. They prodded Red Rock back inside where he hissed and snorted and feigned charges at the crowd, every man, woman and child pressed up against the screen or the fence, jeering and pointing and giving the bull the finger and cursing, "You ain't shit, you big chocolate cocksucker," screaming anything that came to mind at the killer bull. It was then that I noticed some of the drunker Mexicans were crying because Legs had done it. Legs Maldonado had ridden Red Rock.

Rats

The generic term "big wall" indicates any sweep of rock so sheer and so tall it takes days, sometimes weeks to climb. There are exceptions, but genuine big walls almost always have too few holds for free climbing—for hauling yourself up using the rope and attending gear only as a backup, to check a fall should feet or hands fail. A dated illustration of a big wall climber is the one served up by Hollywood, where the burly mountaineer, like a gnat on the side of a skyscraper, slowly and precariously hammers his way up the overhanging rock, stepping from one creaky piton to the next. He looks much the same as the mad pioneers who first bashed their way up the great cliffs in the Italian Dolomites and French Alps, around 1900. The mechanics have evolved a long way in a century; but I wonder if the few climbers who made a trade of climbing big walls in the mid-seventies weren't as crazy as their soul mates who climbed ninety-five years before them, when the boots were hob-nailers and the pitons soft iron, when the hemp ropes weren't worth a shit and routinely snapped during falls.

The most accessible and most popular—and arguably the finest—big walls are in Yosemite Valley, in central California. Since the late fifties, climbers have come from all over the world to climb Half Dome, Sentinel, Leaning Tower, Washington Column, Mt. Watkins, and especially El Capitan, which rises 3,300 feet directly off the scree, and is a marvel to look at and a miracle to climb. Several miles from El Capitan is a tract of dirt, pinon pine and scattered boulders known as Camp 4. It is a dusty and filthy ghetto, and all Yosemite climbers stay there. A mile across the valley is Sentinel. In the early morning and late afternoon, when the sun is lost behind the valley's mile-high rim, Sentinel looks like a 1,600-foot grey tombstone.

I lived in Camp 4 for eight summers, and though during that time I climbed more than twenty walls, I never considered myself an authentic "wall rat." I'd knock off two, perhaps three a year. A wall rat might do ten. And not the "trade routes" like El Capitan's Nose, where the going is straightforward and a fit free climber can really make time. A wall rat thrives on routes where the cracks are like breaks in an old mirror, where nearly every piton hangs three-quarters of the way out of its slot, where there are no cracks at all and you must hook dimples and scallops and bash malleable copper and aluminum swedges into seams and pin scars, where a single rope length might take eight hours to complete, and the whole climb, twelve days.

I didn't have the patience, or the mind, to do anything but dabble with these big-time "nail ups." Although leading scared me, it was doable, lost as I was in the function. Belaying, however—tending the leader's rope, stranded in slings for days at a go—drove me crazy. The intensity of the belay is made so by the long silences. Once the leader is seventy-five feet out, you have to scream to hear each other. You're essentially alone, too much alone. A couple days of that and I had "summit fever," the overmastering desire to get off the climb—and that's just when a wall rat would hit his stride.

When wall climbing reached its peak during the mid-seventies, Camp 4 was divided between the wall rats and the free climbers. We free climbers outnumbered the rats twenty to one: proof, they reckoned, that they were the genuine article, since in any community it's always the few who do the crucial work. There were never many rats. Their craft was too dangerous and required too much suffering. Exposed as they were to sun and wind and long nights dangling in hammocks lashed high above the rest of us, they nonetheless lived in a somewhat sheltered world. Their crusade—if you could call it one—had slowly turned in upon itself since Royal Robbins and the boys first climbed the first wall, the northwest face of Half Dome, in 1957. In the ensuing fifteen years the rats had become increasingly detached and self-contained, finding security and even safety of a kind in the yawning void that the rest of us would pass through only at the fastest possible speed. In a very real way their game was a drama in which they held fast to their outlandish roles, and seemed as bound by the fatalities of fortune as protagonists in a classical play.

They called us free climbers "cuties" and "lightweights," athletic enough, but lacking the essential steel to manage days, sometimes weeks, stapled to a big cliff. Yet they were always goading us to join them on some grim wall.

Many of us were wall climbers—on a limited scale, granted— but rarely did a season pass when a hardcore Yosemite climber didn't slug up a couple of walls. So the rats' needling—which for me started the second I showed up in late May and continued till the moment I left in August—had a grating, cumulative effect because it was not strictly true. If I said as much, the rats would really pipe up.

"Fact is, Long, you're a woose," some rat would inform me.

"And a faggot."

"At least he knows it."

"Fuck all you rats."

"Them are pretty big words, coming from a queeb like you." The rats were not politically correct, and their persistent jeering and hazing led to more than a few fist fights—which were serious affairs considering that most climbers were young, extremely fit and a little crazy to begin with.

"If you were half a man, you'd saddle up with us."

And they'd start waxing poetic about some giant new climb up some giant wall that I knew damn well would embrace great suffering and labor and terror—for me anyway. Then they'd bad mouth and dress me down a little more. No matter how badly my fingers were slashed or my elbows throbbed from too much free climbing, I could almost always brush them off. But if I was reckless enough to let my pride get caught up in the whole affair, if I felt I was losing too much face, I'd call their bluff (in fact, they'd called mine), and I'd find myself bashing up a wall with a couple of rats. Twice I got suckered because I couldn't sufficiently recall the epic I'd had the first time around—when a projected four days turned into eight; when I took a sixty foot fall; when we ran out of food and water the last two days and our urine turned brown and my vitals ached for a month afterward; when I wished my parents had never met and I swore off climbing forever.

Many rats were extravagant characters I liken to the wandering prospectors of the Old West—fiercely private and independent. They cared little for supposed glory, nothing at all for fame. Having their exploits publicized or praised was considered poor form because their game was like all obsessions: personal. However much they liked the hazards, toils and long silences on the high crag, their climbing went beyond liking in almost all directions. What made them rats was who they became when they were pasted high above the world. A few were rich, rebelling against comfortable limits; most of them were poor. They all did just a little better on the walls than on the ground.

Most rats had their share of things going wrong, and they all seemed to come from the ground. So they'd jump onto a wall and for a week or ten days could get free of the ground, and the ground with them. Eventually, the walls became their natural homes and their appointed refuge from a world that confused or annoyed them. A few were different. They loved the ground, but the high crag even more. Zorba the Greek used to dance to forget the pain. Yet when he was happy, he danced just the same. I think if there had been a high crag in Greece, Zorba would have been a wall rat.

Necessity determined that they'd haul duct-taped water bottles, porta-ledges and hammocks, Gortex rain-flys spangled with patches, ensolite pads and sleeping bags with names sewn into them (rarely their own). They also hauled boxes of Milky Ways they'd pinched from the lodge store, and they hauled cans of peaches in heavy syrup, tuna in spring water, greasy foot-long salamis and summer sausages, Pop Tarts, smoked oysters, Cracker Jacks, jelly beans and Life Savers to slacken "Kalahari Throat." And sodas that would explode when opened but cut through the gum that accumulated in your mouth after a days' climbing and so were treasured like diamonds. But it was the other things they hauled that said who they were.

Ron was an extraterrestrial buff, and he hauled pseudo-scientific texts about flying saucers and alien sex. He'd also haul a pair of "4-D" glasses, ludicrous red plastic jobs he had paid serious money for that any sane man could have bought at a joke store for a buck. Through these glasses he could "see" the gaseous trails of Venusian ships. Canadians Hugh and Steve were two of the best rats in the business. One time (along with three cases of Moosehead beer) they hauled a bag of golf balls they'd filched off a driving range in Palm Springs. They teed up on El Cap Tower, a spacious, flat ledge about 2,200 up the cliff. Along with 200 golf balls, they'd brought a three-iron, a driver and a thatch of Astro-Turf, and they spent a June afternoon banging great drives into the meadow below. Several cars were struck, windshields shattered. The rangers closed the road down for three hours, and fanned out on horseback looking for a sniper. Cars backed up, overheated, rammed each other. Tourists fought. There were several arrests. The case was never solved.

Before he died soloing on Higher Cathedral, Joe hauled a hibachi up Half Dome and up Mt. Watkins. Russ hauled a small acetylene torch so he could "barbecue" franks. Along with half-gallons of Diet Coke, Charles hauled up a dozen frisbees and hurled one off the wall every night. When he finally ran out, he grew bored, and led the last 900 feet of an extremely difficult new climb in half a day.

Jeff hauled a brass crucifix and a wallet photo of the Virgin, a fake Spanish doubloon, a slingshot and fifty marbles. I don't know why he hauled these things, or what he did with them. Bernie soloed the Leaning Tower and Half Dome wearing a yarmulke—partly from authentic devotion, partly because he was "so bald you could see his thoughts." Tom hauled a harmonica, a kazoo and a ten-pound ghetto blaster on which he'd play the soundtrack from "Doctor Zhivago" till we were ready to murder him—and we would have if he hadn't gone six-foot three, two and a quarter.

They traded off hauling the bags, sharing the weight of strange lives, dragging up the wall what others did not want, including each other. They hauled the clouds and the rain and the sun pounding on their heads. They hauled thirst that would have killed a camel. Before an avalanche swept him off Mount Kenya, Dan hauled a medical degree up El Capitan. Others hauled scabies and the drip, smashed fingers and swollen feet, broken ribs and broken hearts. One rat hauled leukemia up El Capitan at least three times that I know of. They scattered his ashes over Washington Column from a Stearman biplane.

They hauled the very mountain, shards of it flaking off under 10,000 hammer blows and sticking to their faces and necks and hands, stinging their eyes, blinding them to everything below. They hauled the pull of the earth and they hauled the earth itself because they could never leave it completely behind.

Take Darrel, known affectionately as "Cro-Magnon," a Canadian wood-cutter and the most stalwart bastard ever to swing a piton hammer. He had one buck tooth and a face like a cigar-store Indian. His fractured speech was the most conspicuous proof that he was self-educated. If he wasn't, his teachers should have been flogged. He seemed to survive exclusively on malt whisky and "branch water," as he called it, and at the wee hours he could always be found stumbling back into Camp 4 with a load on. The next morning, it was straight back to the hair of the dog that bit him. Whenever he had a little more liquor on board than usual, some fellow rat would drag him off to El Cap, Half Dome, or Mt. Watkins. It'd take him several days to dry out and hit his stride. The second he did, he wanted off the wall and he wanted liquor so he'd take over all the leading and climb furiously to get the business over with. By the time the team would "top out," Cro-Magnon was in mint condition, while his partners looked like they'd just crossed Death Valley on bare knees. Then it was straight to the liquor store for Cro-Magnon, then back onto a wall, then back into the bottle and it was just one crazy, endless go-around.

They hauled the stress of men engaged in dangerous work and they made jokes about it. They hauled their honor with them, for they were its only custodians. Some hauled loneliness so deep and so treasured they would share it with no one—like "Private Dave" from Montana, thirty-something and heroically laconic, who always climbed his walls solo, which is twice as dangerous, three times the work and a hundred times more frightening. (If any man should feel like the last soul on earth, he's the one hanging alone in a hammock in the dead of night, half a mile up a big wall.) After a long climb, Dave would join in at every campfire, laugh and carouse with climbers he'd known for ten years. Then, slowly, we'd see less and less of him, until finally he'd start laying out gear on a tarp and borrowing water bottles. And where was Dave going? "Back to the high lonesome," he'd say, grim as a hangman, "Where there ain't no people at all—yet." "Private Dave" preferred his own company, and up on the high lonesome, he and the work understood each other perfectly.

The sun and moon would come and go but time was frozen for the rats. They climbed a foot a minute—maybe—working toward the sky, hammering, always hammering, beyond will power and resolve because it was all instinct, an emptying of thought. They had no commission and no guarantees, no boss and no pay. They took insane risks. They'd wander over vast oceans of vertical rock, seemingly with no scheme or objective, because the yawning void was their overriding purpose. Their quest was their religion, and in religion seeking is finding. In other ventures, it's the object of the quest that often brings satisfaction, or something incidental picked up along the way. But in the rat's theology, desire was fulfillment, so to travel hopefully was better than to arrive. The summit meant nothing, the wall everything.

Eventually, some rats moved on to big mountains in Peru and Bolivia and Tibet and India and China, and many of them never made it back. Over time, the others ran out of frisbees and golf balls, tired of Cracker Jacks and Doctor Zhivago, could no longer see anything through their red plastic glasses, could no longer haul a world of their own making. By twos and threes, the rats left Yosemite and for many years, the walls were nearly silent.

They were the genuine article. They hauled life and death in the same bag. We called them wall rats and they hauled with them a dream now lost in time, like the slipstreams of Venusian ships.

Mr. Doom

Four months before he arrived in country, Dirk's military history had been written by Lt. Colonel Robert A. Dunston. That in the madness and chaos it played out almost completely to Dunston's plan was part miracle, part nightmare, for never was there a more fatal clash of aspirations.

From what he told me, Dirk's father had been a Marine during the Second World War, so with a new fight underway, signing up was required of him. He'd grown up kicking around the Montana woods, and was a fixture at the local rifle range. He started competing at age eight, working from small bore, to high-powered, on to rapid fire service rifle, and finally to 1,000-meter match competition. At fifteen, he won his first of four state championships. Never much for hunting, he mostly liked to target shoot. At boot camp, his gunplay so astounded his C.O. that the second he was through—and despite being disciplined thirteen times for shenanigans—he was dealt into advanced infantry training, and later, into a marksmanship unit. The Marines still didn't know what they had until he entered the 1,000-yard National High-Powered Rifle Championship at Camp Perry—the Wimbledon Cup. It was impossible that a teenager should win. But everything about Dirk Patrick Novak was impossible, and he won going away. His C.O. was so pissed off that Dirk competed wearing cut-off camo pants and a little fuck-you hat that he denied him his sergeant stripes, and shipped him off to Asia as a corporal. He was nineteen years old. Just turned, I think.

Dirk was a natural for the 4rd Marine Division's Scout/Sniper squadron. We were eighteen men. Dunston was our commanding officer, but insisted that he never actually meet Dirk, and so far as I know he never did. Always lingering in the shadows, he pretty much left the day-to-day calls up to me. I was 23 then, from Louisiana. Twenty-six months before I was in the graduate lit program at LSU, mainly blowing weed and cocking around. I was also in ROTC to make sure I never left Louisiana. Then they started that goddam draft lottery, rolling the dice with people's lives. I drew number 21, was in boot camp five weeks later, then straight into the fire. I knew a thing or two about guns and was a little older than most of the other guys, and just fell into the rest after our sergeant got his legs blown off in Quangtri.

I'd heard about Dirk before he showed up in Chu Lai—about his shooting, anyway—and so expected someone other than the kid with the confiding blue eyes and the bounce in his step who waltzed off that C-130 transport. Every sniper from every fire team received orientation from Cedric Riley, a chump with soupy grey eyes who pretended to the rank of gunnery sergeant. Slovenly, smelling of stale beer, Riley rarely left his Quonset hut, cowering under his desk when the rain fell too hard, and goading the recruits into a cataclysm he neither suffered or understood. One of the tragedies of the whole debacle is that of the oceans of spilled blood, none of it was Riley's. Along with Dirk, two other recruits were assigned to me, and the four of us met with Riley straightaway. The two others were all raw nerves and red eyes from the seventeen-hour flight from San Diego. Not so Dirk, who strode into Riley's office like he owned the place.

"This baby's shit-canned," Dirk said, thumping the swamp cooler chattering on the wall. "I'd go with a couple locals and a palm frond," he laughed.

"Lose the hat, corporal" Riley barked. Dirk lost his hat and started fanning himself with it as Riley launched into his spiel, the same one I'd heard two years before, and had hung my heart on every fatuous word. Riley only got about three sentences into it this time.

"Christ, sarge," Dirk cut in, still fanning himself, "I need a stint in the meat locker, where you guys keep all the filets." Riley flushed, and yelled, "How's that, Corporal?"

Dirk flashed that disarming smile, where you could see almost all of his teeth. Then he extended his hand and said, "I'm new to all this, Gunney. And my wires are crossed from all that flying. But I'm looking to be an able jarhead, sir, if you'll have me."

Riley was confounded. He slowly shook Dirk's hand.

"So what 'da you say we just skip all the boot camp hogwash and get over to that meat locker?" Dirk laughed.

Dirk was lucky—lucky in a certain way, that is. Riley had no real clout. All the officers thought him a fool. Had Riley been anybody else, Dirk would have been dragged off to latrine duty and wouldn't have got off the pot till the monsoon came, if then. The corps builds its regulars by smashing the identities they brought with them. But Dirk lived with a buoyancy that seemed bulletproof. The rules that applied to the rest of us could not and never would concern Corporal Dirk Novak.

"Just get him out of here," the Sergeant muttered to me. On Riley's door was the slogan: "Adversity does not break men, it makes men."

"What's that fella do for a living, anyhow?" Dirk asked once we were outside.

I led Dirk and the other two recruits over to our hooch, dug into a calving mud hillside overlooking "Tiger Valley," our field of operations. Inside, half a dozen of my men were waiting to meet America's best shot, not the blue-eyed rogue who burst through the tin door.

"Nice digs," Dirk laughed. The place was a dump. Even the dirt walls were sweating. "Hell, you'd have to set a mortar in here with wiener tongs. Yeah, this will do," he said, whisking some gear off my bunk and onto the floor. Then he plopped down and was out in about ten seconds.

Dirk Novak had a genius for mimicking superiors—a little lisp, a twitch, even the way the colonel scratched his ass. Medals or age meant nothing to him, and even generals loved him for it. He had the gift of simple and moving expression, and since every face was an open book to him, he mocked us all, none more than the chopper pilots. He passed his first month in Tiger Valley serving a kind of apprenticeship, mainly observing. They usually threw grunts straight into the fire, but Dunston wanted to groom the best shot in America, figuring if we kept him alive long enough to understand things, he'd pay dividends once he held out his hand to the flame. Virtually every night, choppers would blade out on recons, and pilots were always begging Dirk along.

"Me? In those rattle-traps?" he'd laugh. "Too many moving parts. The hamster dies and a thousand hearts are broke in Montana."

"She-it" would ring from the pilots.

"And get it right, hayseed," one of them would say, "it takes a genius to keep that hamster going."

Dirk would choke and say, "If you guys were any dumber, I'd have to water you." And they'd all holler and bicker some more. But most every night, Dirk would stumble from the hooch in those asinine cut-offs and that fuck-you hat and wander down to the landing zone. "Better see what's doing with those fools." Then he'd jump aboard and they would blade off into the long night, Dirk on the door gun, blazing away. Having Dirk along, the pilots felt they were free of danger for the rest of their lives— which averaged about three weeks in a hot zone.

"That kid's like a rabbit's foot," one would say. "Guys like him never get scratched."

His enormous skill as a marksman gave him great license, but the cut-offs and the hat could not be allowed. More importantly, they were dangerous for a sniper, who has enough people gunning for him without "marking" himself with idiotic gear. I told Dirk as much. Lieutenants screamed at him. Captains did everything but lock him up. And he still wore the cut-offs and he still wore the hat. "What are they gonna do, Sarge? Sack me?" And he'd laugh, so I could see all his teeth. I told him he was going to get himself greased and he said "No chance in hell, Sarge. I was born lucky."

After a month, our little hooch was always packed. Rank accounted for nothing in there, and buck privates and decorated officers and Marines of every race and color would quarrel and howl at Dirk's ridiculing of everything and everybody, disparaging the crazy chances and dangers we all endured and recounting them in mock terror.

"I could have died out there" he'd scream into a lieutenant's face, "And I got hussies, see—"

"Boy, you couldn't get laid with a thousand dollar bill." And off we'd go. Some raged, some cried, and a few took a swing at him; but every ear was tuned to the blond-haired kid who spoke our secrets openly, who made us believe our lives counted for something, if only in that grubby little hooch. I think it was because Dirk's behavior was so superbly inappropriate that it somehow worked—or maybe his unique magic made it work—and we all joined in his kind of alternative insanity, laughing in a bottomless pit. He reminded many of us of what we'd lost, and people hung around just hoping something of the kid might rub off on them. But we were all soul dead and hell bound, and slowly, something of the crowd, and the cancerous method of the place, started rubbing off on him.

The particulars varied, but mostly he'd slither through the bush and gun a man down at distance, a thing I'd done thirty-one times over twenty-seven months. Yet even when I had to go I.D. the corpse, the foul truth of the trade never totally sunk in. What with the danger, terror and exhaustion, there wasn't time to think anything through. I'd get around to that several wives later, once the blood dried and the hurdle became life itself.

Dirk was different. He knew from the start what he was doing, what it all meant. The generals were proud of their "assassins." But both the title and the trade dealt death to the kid with the bounce in his step. Still, he kept on, faithfully doing his job, hauled along by the nameless spirit of combat, racked by our "success" and disgusted by all the pat bilge pumped into us from day one: The proviso is old as war itself—that you kill a man, woman, or even a child because they will kill your best friend, then you. You get caught in a fire fight and it's easy to justify killing someone. He tried to kill you. If you attacked, he could fight or surrender. You didn't murder him. He fought back, and he lost. That's self defense, the credo ran. But the sniper's code demolished this logic. We didn't want anybody fighting back, and we honored no white flag. Any way we tried to dress it up or defend it, we were still committing premeditated murder on strangers—if we stopped and thought about it. Dirk Novak thought about it. Then he'd do it again. It was like the work had grabbed him by the short hairs and never let go. Not for a minute.

We usually went out in pairs. The spotter had a tripod-mounted scope and a M-16 just in case. The sniper shot a 7.62 caliber model 700 Remington, with a Special Redfield 3-to-9 scope and a range-finding radical. One hundred and seventy-three grain boat-tailed bullets did the job when they found their mark, and Dirk could find it like no other. In only six months, he had ninety-seven confirmed kills, though he'd probably greased half again that many. And everyone knew it. Dirk Novak, the deadliest Marine in hell, was an instant legend. By his own hand he'd been baptized in the same blood we all were drowning in, and it'd be some months before I would understand just why, and for whom, he did it. His eyes slowly filled with shattered light and inside our hooch, Dirk's audience quickly vanished.

After each foray, Dirk brought more of the jungle's hungry silence back to the wire with him. He rarely spoke anymore, which was just as well; but whenever he did talk it was with the forbearance of a priest in a confessional. It both enchanted and shot through us like a spear, because prowling behind the hushed voice, the graceful moving hands and the timid, lowered eyes was an indomitable killer. The contrast petrified those who had been around him from day one. People had problems sleeping in the same hooch with him, to say nothing of joining him on patrol.

So we went out together: me spotting, Dirk shooting. Sometimes when Dirk and me would go I.D. a dead VC, certain Marines would carve off ears and do other gruesome things. Dirk had been in country roughly seven months, with about one hundred kills when he started sticking water lilies in the wounds of his victims—as a trademark or some black requiem, I do not know. I only know that after gunning a man down, it was a very odd gesture.

With each passing week, Dirk grew more invincible, more monstrous, more polite, and less human—a sort of Cerberus gone amok. He was the stone dropped into the red pool, the impulses sending grim ripples through the whole compound and beyond. Our blue-eyed hope was dead. Behind his back, people started calling him "Mr. Doom." It had taken only eight months.

Eventually, he barely spoke at all, even to me. During debriefings, he talked in a whisper you could barely hear, and always with that ghastly politeness that had nothing remotely military about it, and, in fact, countered Marine decorum more than the jesting he strolled off the C-130 with. The de-brief brass were accustomed to—and expected—tales of courage and honor and grit, and so to hear a VC with a sucking chest wound described with almost religious unction caught them totally off guard (and turned more than one career officer the very color of ashes). Dirk would excuse himself, slink back to the hooch, clean his weapon and stare at the mud walls, leaving the officers in ghostly silence, wondering if they hadn't just seen Satan in human form.

Some maintained, correctly, that Dirk was disrupting morale; others thought him preternaturally weird, still others, stone-cold mad. Whatever he was, he was not one of the Few Good Men, never had been and never could be now. Several suggested easing him out of the corps, but in the shadows, Lt. Colonel Dunston decided something else. He started sending him out on special missions. Alone.

They'd chopper him, say, to the Laotian border, where he'd grease a Chink advisor, or a VC general, or whoever INTEL wanted greased. At the start they sent a land-nav ace along with him—some guy who could cross Borneo with a compass and a bag of rice cakes. But Dirk had grown up outdoors, had learned the jungle like a song and so after the second mission, he was allowed to go it alone. If there was ever a dicier job in war, I don't know it. Everybody knew these missions were suicidal, yet Dirk always came crawling back to our wire, sometimes weeks later, trembling with malaria, starving, ravished by rip-saw vines or busted up from a helicopter crash, but in a few weeks he was back on his feet. Some horrendous force drove him. It was not of him, but it owned him body and soul.

There were other fiends, like Tyron Dell, a kid from Arkansas with a tight little grin and grey eyes too close together, who would go out on patrol and stay out until he found two VCs sacked out. He'd slash the throat of one, leaving the other to wake up and find his dead partner. Guys like Tyron were always yapping about their work and you secretly knew they were terrified. Dirk rarely said a word, and when he did it was always with that chilling civility. His attitude was the very opposite of most

Marines', who were buckling from the loss of control and personal power, haunted by the arbitrary round or mine that could send them back home in a satchel. You suspected that Dirk never got rattled by any of it, that some unknowable part of him thrived on the uncertainty, was grateful for it. And that was scary. Toward the end, his face mirrored on a lurid scale what seethed below the surface in all of us, and people would dash into the latrine or even go out on patrol to avoid seeing him.

He stopped talking altogether, or so infrequently it amounted to the same thing. He'd become extremely valuable to the high command, who'd long given up on trying to whip the VC, handcuffed as they were by Washington. Their only satisfaction was to menace and infuriate the enemy, and Mr. Doom was their man. He knew far too much—secret, unauthorized stuff—to be mingling with regulars, or anyone else. He'd wasted dozens of key VC leaders, then slipped through their clasping fists like water through a sieve. And it enraged them. They spread word to every shit hole in every jungle nook. They dropped flyers and put up a king's ransom for the blond-haired devil who stuck water lilies in the wounds of their slain comrades. That he should get captured and interrogated was unthinkable. So after every mission, he was spirited away to a safe house in Da Nang and kept under armed guard. And everyone at camp breathed a little easier.

INTEL thought he might crack if the VC ever caught and tortured him, so they marched him through a battery of tests, the same ones they used on Marines afraid of their shadows, who heard voices, who'd seen God or thought they were God, who'd shot their own lieutenants or a VC village full of women and kids. But they couldn't touch the tortured core of a man—that didn't concern them anyway—so Dirk was pronounced "mentally sound." He thoroughly rankled one fool doctor who tried to hypnotize him, though.

"You're pretty smart for someone whose next life looms so—imminently," the doctor said.

"Wrong, sawbones," Dirk said, his eyes like a beast of prey. "A man without a shadow lives forever." The doctor signed him off, I think mainly just to give his prediction a chance. Only then did I realize that Dirk had evolved into a closing phase. The manners were gone now. It was all Mr. Doom.

The Viper put Dirk back in Chu Lai for his last mission. In a hot driving rain, a chopper dumped him off near Hill 29, the Sniper squadron's base of operations 60 miles east of Da Nang. I met him at the LZ. There was sporadic incoming, so we jogged to the hooch, a new one overlooking Tiger Valley, where we were having all the trouble.

The valley and the quadrant beyond it was our Tactical Area of Responsibility, and troops routinely marched through it. All told, in and around the valley, and in only three months, forty-eight Marines had fallen to a VC sniper known as The Viper. The Marines could live with losing thirty-four grunts, but The Viper had killed six officers as well. Then he'd gunned down a full-bird colonel, and the brass said enough. The Viper also had greased seven of my snipers, and we couldn't figure out how to snare him, save by clearing the troops out and carpet bombing the entire valley—something suggested by one crazy general (who later was cleared of war crimes he'd actually ordered).

The Viper was the VC's comeback to Mr. Doom, and blowing that colonel away—an insulting piece of work done right in the compound at flaming high noon—was a kind of grim reckoning, an open dare for the blond-haired devil to come and have at it, if he thought he could. Of course, it'd been some months since Dirk had gone out on the kind of patrols where he'd ever meet The Viper. Like I said, I think they were mainly heli-inserting him into Laos and along the Cambodian border, alone. When he'd gotten his man and thrashed back, it was straight into the armed safe house in Da Nang. Now The Viper was trying to lure him out. Actually, I doubt Dirk ever heard much, if anything, about The Viper. But Lt. Colonel Dunston had. So he called Dirk in.

Inside the hooch, I told Dirk all I knew, or what I'd heard anyway, since no one had actually seen The Viper—that he lived in the meanest jungle, that he caught kraits and king cobras with his bare hands and ate them raw so he could have their spirit in him. The VC had cooked up a bunch of other crap about how he could hear an ant breathe, and see in the dark, and make himself change colors like a chameleon, and was immortal. We only knew for sure that he was stealthy and a deadly shot and that if he caught you alone, or nailed you and your partner—which happened numerous times—he'd slice your forehead to the bone and peel the hide right off your face (More than once, he'd done this when the Marine was still alive). I found four of my men like this and I still see what was left in my sleep. The morning's briefing had The Viper creeping around a rampart of primary jungle at the head of Tiger Valley. A dawn patrol found two very dead Black Berets up there that confirmed The Viper's strike: shot through the head from long range, faces skinned. Victims forty-nine and fifty.

Dirk said nothing, just kept smearing black camo grease over his face and legs, something he'd started these last few months. Seeing those blue eyes peering through that black mask made my flesh crawl. You could sense something living and human behind those eyes, but all I could see was Mr. Doom, and he was death, death minus all the flags and poetry and priestcraft, the absolute, final extinction in rotting corpses and maggots. I could smell it, taste it, and it hardened in my gut like quick-set cement. Who knows what was going through his mind? He was going after The Viper. That was all.

The whole stinking disaster was virtually over and I know Dunston was wondering what the hell they'd do with Dirk when we officially quit the place altogether. Because The Viper had bagged so many so fast, his reputation seemed almost mythical, and a lot of Marines and even the brass considered him invincible. Whatever else Dunston thought, I'm certain he figured The Viper would eliminate the Dirk question for him. A nice, clean getaway for Dunston. Dirk said we might as well get going. I didn't know whether to be flattered or terrified that Dirk wanted me along. Two days later, I regretted having gone with him more than anything I'd ever done. We'd found The Viper—or he'd found us—and we'd been running ever since. He moved through the jungle like a spirit and had a starving leopard's instinct about where we were, or were heading. I tried keeping him at range with bursts from my M-16, but he was too wily to hit. He was behind, then in front of us, then he was everywhere at once. He'd gotten off several shots, and had grazed Dirk in the thigh. Dirk hadn't squeezed a single shot off. For the first time I knew I was way over my head. After two days, my mind was gone.

Now, we were dug in behind a rotten banyan log. Peering out through dense ferns and elephant grass, we could see that the slope below dropped away in a tangled riot of jungle where a rhinoceros could hide and you'd never see it. Rain pattered down, and the thick mulch reeked and steamed around us. The Viper was down there somewhere, had us pinned, our backs to a little overgrown bluff. I thought we might survive till dawn, maybe longer, but there was no exit, no way out. And The Viper was down there, grinning, chewing on lizards and rats and listening to ants breathe for all I knew, waiting to flick his tongue out at two flies. We were dead men, and knew it. Or I did anyway. First I raged, then prayed it might pass, then silently wept because I knew it wouldn't, and finally I begged for it to happen fast. Nothing stirred, not a sound but the bugs and the stewing vegetation, which made the waiting worse.

At midnight, illumination rounds started popping way overhead, tumbled through the clouds and glimmered off patches of flooded paddy a mile below. In the checkered glow I now and then caught the flash of Dirk's eyes, welded to a vague patch of jungle a hundred yards below. He never spoke, didn't move, didn't blink, just kept his eyes on that blurry spot of thicket. I was exhausted and scared shitless and had to close one eye to focus on anything. We hadn't eaten in two days. I sort of zoned out a couple times but snapped to at dawn.

Dirk's eyes were still zeroed on that vague patch. A mortal battle was going on but it was so far beyond me that I couldn't fathom the real texture of it—just an inkling of feints and ruses between two fatal immensities. Trapped between them, my heart slammed in my chest because as Dirk went, so would I. And we were had.

The sun popped up so fast it seemed to hit me right between the eyes. I got behind the spotting scope but didn't see anything, and hadn't for three days. The crushing silence was the worst part. "Now we know what it's like," Dirk finally said. Yes, we now knew about being stalked by a sudden peremptory force that could strike like lightning and blow us straight to hell. I thought about all those we'd pinned down—like when a patrol of VC, spooked by unseen shots, would desperately flee for a tree or a river, and how we'd plunk them off like ducks on a pond. The terror and hopelessness they must have felt—we knew all about it now. There were no white flags, had never been any apologies, but just then I was the sorriest man on earth. And mad, raving mad that the jackass who had committed us to this war wasn't pinned down behind that log. I'd killed dozens of men but it was his dirty work I was doing, and the bastard deserved to be squirming and sweating his balls off there more than I did.

Then I spotted something, a point of light from that vague spot below. "You see that?" I whispered. Dew drops on a leaf could glint like this, but when I glanced over at Dirk, he already had his rifle leveled on the trunk and was sighting on that point of light. He simply said, "Get down." I rolled flat behind the log and stared up at him. He exhaled, letting the cross hairs settle, and his features relaxed so totally that I saw a dead man's face. I'd seen that face dozens, hundreds of times and it always looked the same. Then Dirk squeezed off his first and only shot, the report ripping down the slope and cracking out across the paddy. There was a sickening meat sound—whether the round had struck The Viper or the moist pulp of a tree, I didn't know. I peered over the log. No glint. No sound. Nothing.

Dirk slowly stood up, tore his shirt off and started wiping the black camo grease off his face. I was baffled and burnt out, but Dirk was wide open now, and completely gave away our position. "What the hell you doing?" I begged him.

Dirk ignored me, or was oblivious, as he slowly scrambled over to the edge of the limestone bluff and traversed along a thin ledge to where he had an unobstructed view of the entire valley, spread out a mile below. We were in the thick of it, but over the last few months the landscape below had taken so much mortar fire that, aside from a few sad paddies, the whole valley was charred and cratered and looked like Hades with the flames turned off. I lay rigid behind the log, my mind racing, gaping up at Dirk and wincing, seeing his face with the flesh peeled off it, waiting for the blast of The Viper's rifle, my hands over my head to shield the shower of gore that would surely come. I prayed for it, the brain shot that would break his allegiance to obscenity and evil, that would mercifully blow away the kid's pain. For that one moment, I didn't even care if I was next. But there was only that crushing silence as Dirk gazed over the valley, his eyes on infinity.

The same hurry of my mind, like a man falling through air,would not let me sort through the moment; but the hum of insects above the otherwise funereal silence snapped me out of it. Finally, Dirk wandered back from the rock, stepped over the log and started hiking down below. I grabbed my A-16, stepped over the defilade and followed him down the slope toward where that glimmer had been. The thought of being pinned down again, strangled by the feeling of total hopelessness, frightened me more than death as we dropped one, two-hundred yards before we stopped. And there was The Viper, slumped back on some cane leaves.

All the images my mind had styled about him—while pacing in the hooch, while humping another faceless victim in from patrol, while squirming behind the banyan log, my teeth gnashing and my heart hammering through my chest—all these images were wrong.

The Viper was just a kid. Fourteen, maybe fifteen, with red and black serpents tattooed about his neck. His only garment was a black loincloth. The rest of his body was smeared with green camo grease, and wrapped in leaves and bits of roots and twigs. For a long time, we just looked at him lying there, waiting for him to change colors or spring back to life.

Finally I reached down to a little scabbard lashed to his leg and pulled the knife out, a skinner's knife, sharp as death. I found his gun nearby, a Russian Mosin-Nangant 7.62. I picked it up and peered down the long, hollow PU scope. The glass had been blown out of it by Dirk's bullet, which had whizzed through The Viper's right eye and blown the back of his head off. The glimmering we'd seen had been the sun playing off The Viper's scope as he'd sighted on us. Dirk had simply beat The Viper to the shot.

No one I had ever seen or even heard about could move through the jungle like this child warrior. We'd been overmatched in open jungle. Dirk knew it, and had simply backed against a rock and reduced the hunt to a shooting match. And the devil himself couldn't beat Mr. Doom in a shooting match.

Dirk stood there, teetering, staring at The Viper. Something had totally changed with him, so gutted, so lonely and forever did he now look. His mouth slowly came open, wider and wider, and for several minutes he remained like that, so wobbly he had to lean against his gun to stay standing, drooling out the sides of his mouth. It started as a low, guttural droning that slowly gave way to the cries of two-hundred murdered men echoing from the black hole inside of him, pouring out his open mouth like a lava flow. I'll never be able to explain it but we were suddenly surrounded by the ghosts of all the men we'd killed—dozens of them just drifted in from the shadows. I recognized the one, the first of Dirk's many victims, a fine-boned boy, maybe twenty, in a grimy black shirt and grimy black pajama pants, there on his knees with a baffled look, both hands holding links of gleaming blue entrails spilling from his belly, ripped open by a burst from Dirk's A-16. Around him, the others wept and raged and shook with terror and bled and slumped and finally ebbed away till all that survived of them was our intractable sense of shame and dishonor and loneliness.

"I did it for them, but I didn't know," he said, "I didn't know what it was like." That's all he said, but he had told me everything.

Through all these harrowing months he'd never forgotten those who used to flood our little hooch, and who later hid from the monster he'd become. Every mission Dirk fought had been "for them." In his twisted heart, selling his soul to Mr. Doom was an act of love for the many who used to huddle round the blond-haired ace who verified their lives. He'd gone out alone, to spare us, to save us. Ultimately, it was the only hope he could give. But the story of those fleeting ghosts, the ghastly price of his sacrifice—that part he couldn't have known. All these things I realized in an instant.

By late afternoon we'd stumbled back to the wire. I gave a quick breakdown to Dunston, and I don't think till that very instant did he realize the measure of the monster he'd created. He acted like he couldn't believe it but mostly he didn't want to believe it—that for practical purposes we were finished in Asia and he still had Dirk on his hands, that his sure-fire solution, the immortal Viper, was lying on a bed of cane leaves with his brains blown out by Dirk's first and only shot.

I sent out a patrol to retrieve The Viper's body, and Dirk and I retired to the hooch. Dirk slept for most of two days. When he came around, the demon had flown out of him, having consumed both the human and monster. His eyes were clear, but blank, and for several hours he just milled about the hooch in a sort of denatured limbo, another ravaged throwaway, useless to himself and the world. He said he was retired, and laughed. I'll never forget my last memory of him there, an MP at each elbow, marching him onto a CH-46 transport heading for division and the C-130 bound for San Diego. At the cargo door, he stopped and turned around for one last look. His face was a study of confusion. It was impossible then to realize that this gutted shell was the same kid who had waltzed into camp only fourteen months before.

Back in the states they made him a sergeant and pinned a bunch of medals on him, but all the words from all the brass couldn't make him re-up. He was retired, he said, and that was all. They discharged him a few months later. That was twenty years ago and I never saw Dirk again. But all of these years I've been backed up to a wall of rock and cringing behind a banyan log, waiting for a boat-tailed bullet that would blow the memories away.

A Piece of Steel

My first recollections of Mexico are of Humberto Mata's finca in Santa Cruz, dim memories of crags and wind torn plains and sage that slashed my legs when my cousin Faustino and I chased chuckwallas behind an old adobe well. But I remember perfectly the first time Dad and I went to Francisco Orozco's Rancho Piru in Reynoso.

My grandfather, Oscar Mauricio Rincon, had started a cattle ranch shortly after opening his first dental clinic in El Paso in 1928. Dad had grown up on the ranch, and though he had little to do with it anymore, he'd agreed to truck a big stud bull down to Reynoso to get a break from the family restaurant. I joined him for company.

The drive took three hours. I can remember the bull kicking the plate steel walls of the trailer so hard it sounded like mortar fire, and how every thirty minutes, Dad would pull over and toss buckets of water over the bull who was jet black and roasting in the sun and getting more savage with each mile.

In all the district, should you go fifty miles in any direction, you could not find a tree as large as the Piru tree standing alone next to Francisco's finca. It was know as "The Piru," and all of the vast rancho, "Piru." The finca consisted of a low sprawl of cement quartos, darned together with mortar and huge oaken beams garlanded with bougainvillaea and dahlias. A few hundred feet north it was almost all cattle and horses.

At Piru, dad backed the trailer up to a big corral: "Guapo" charged out and froze. Everyone ringed round the fence and started chucking pebbles at the bull. Francisco Orozco had invited a bunch of other beef ranchers—two came all the way from Matamoros—and these men were more excited and threw more pebbles than the dozen or so of us kids. The gringo ranchers I'd been around in Texas were mostly grave businessmen, and you didn't throw so much as a hard look at their livestock. But here in Mexico, as I was beginning to see, people rarely outgrow a passion for simple novelty, so it was unaceptable for big ranchers to have driven all the way to Reynoso to see Guapo just wheezing through his nose ring, not even scratching the ground.

After several minutes, a rancher named Martin Rulfo Moreno—a fiery man with a face like Geronimo—toed his cheroot into the ground, spit for effect, snatched his wife's lap dog and chucked it into the corral. Moreno's wife shrieked as the bull rumbled after the Chihuahua at speed. The dog zipped through the slats, just outdistancing a ton-and-a-half of lunging bull that slammed into the fence with the concussion of a train wreck.

"Jesu Christo," Moreno yelled. He had a mouth full of gold teeth and I could see them all. The other ranchers kept yelling "Eeeejole!" and "Jesu Christo!" and slapping Francisco's back. Moreno's wife cursed him root and branch and gathered her lap dog, kissing it's wet feet. I can still picture this woman, her rouged cheeks, dangling agates and stiletto heels pocking the mud with little exclamation marks as she scampered away, nuzzling that asinine rat dog.

As we moved toward the finca, the women and children, and the men, sort of paired off into two groups. I hadn't been out from under my mother's skirts for so long, and didn't know for sure what group I should fall in with till Dad glanced over and said, "Come on, Carlos." It was my first time within the inner-circle of the men, which has always been a kind of masonic order in Mexico. On the porch, the ranchers scraped manure off their boots with a hoof pick. I gave the same treatment to my tennis shoes, and followed Dad into a big room that Francisco used for an office—with its brass and burl wet bar set up in one corner, and a garish portrait of the Virgin de Guadalupe hanging beside the mirror. Francisco told me to latch the screen behind me to keep the flies out.

It was shady and cool inside the room, and the sharp smell of mescal and ripe lemons hung in the close air. The dozen or so empty bottles on top of the bar told the story. The men were spread over the room in various chairs, and I hung back in the shadows, struggling to understand their quick, guttural Spanish. They drank and they argued in a way I'd never seen before, quick to say what they felt soon as they felt it, now and then romancing the odd detail for theatrical value. I moved over to the wall by the bar and started fingering a shard of gnarled pot iron strung on the end of a rosary. When Francisco came over to fill his glass, he said, "That, Carlitos, is from the revolution. It came from your General Pershing's cannon, nearly killed me and saved my life at the same time." I glanced over at Dad, who smiled drolly.

Francisco was hale and sharp despite his seventy-something years; but the other men weren't buying his revolution bit anymore than dad was. Martin Rulfo Moreno went over and examined the piece of metal, and said, "I believe you have the biggest bull in Sonora, Francisco, but I do not believe you fought in the revolution."

This was nearly twenty years ago, and Francisco Orozco was a big boss back then. He glared at Moreno like he was a pig.

"I was only a boy like Carlitos here and was just trying to get away from that bastard Villa, who had taken our city, as you know. Or maybe you didn't know that," Francisco mocked.

"Villa? Poncho Villa?" Moreno said. "You never saw so much as Poncho Villa's burro, you big brown liar."

"I swear on the sacred heart I saw Villa," Francisco said. "And Villa rode no burro. He rode a big piebald stallion and I saw that too."

"I heard Poncho Villa liked little boys," joked another rancher, Aldolfo de la Rubio, a fat old turd whose stuffed waistcoat had gold lame piping snaking down the arms.

"He liked their blood, I can tell you that," Francisco raged.

"You know Poncho did fight the gringo general, though," said Jesus Rolendez, the only sober man among them. His face, which belonged on a hangman, was splotched by a port wine-stain birthmark. "I read about that," he added.

"And you read correctly," Francisco promised.

"Basura" said yet another rancher named Lopez, whose voice boomed when he wanted it to. He must have lived off atole and bird seed he was so skinny, and I couldn't get over hearing such a big voice coming from that skeleton. "I know for a fact that Poncho Villa never came here, just his men."

"What do you know, Lopez?" Francisco growled. "Do you even know who Venustiano Carranza was? Did you know Carranza fought Villa, not Villa's men but Poncho Villa himself, right here in Reynoso?" Lopez fingered his cigar and blew smoke rings at the ceiling.

"Carranza was kicking Villa's ass because he had more men and supplies than Villa. So that idiot Villa raids a couple Yanqui border towns, and next thing the General Pershing storms into Reynoso and starts blowing everything up looking for Villa."

"And he never found him because Villa was never here," Lopez howled.

"You were still in your father's pecker then, Lopez. You don't know nothing."

"My uncle was born here in Reynoso and he told me Villa never came here, just his men. And I believe my uncle. Have another drink, Francisco."

Francisco scoffed. "Your uncle? That woodcutter. I saw Poncho Villa and I hope to die if I didn't see him. And I saw his men kill half the men in this town. More than half."

I kept following whoever was talking, then back to my Dad— who had a tight little grin on his face—then returned to whoever cut back into the contest. I seemed to be the only one who didn't know who or what to believe.

Rolendez made a sucking sound on the lemon slice in his mouth, hawked it out and fingered his lip. "Villa did kill the men here," Rolendez started, "I read that too, but I don't know about half."

"More than half," Francisco said. "All the men in Reynoso were farmers and none of them wanted any part of Carranza or Villa. But the farmers were forced to enlist. If they refused, the soldiers would cut off the soles of their feet and make them run across the open country, then they would shoot them down. Or they would tie them to the tail of the caballo and drag them over the cobblestones at a gallop. They did this to my cousin Vicente and I saw it. If they needed food and you had none, they would nail the man of the house to the door, or would bury him up to his neck so his head would crack as the melon cracks when the cavalry stampeded over it. Then that half-breed Villa runs out of supplies and raids the gringo border towns and the General Pershing comes down on us like a bull in heat."

"Maybe Pershing was looking for the blood of little boys as well," de la Rubio laughed, the big fat sap jiggling on the stool. "Maybe he did not even care about Poncho."

"Just keep laughing, you picaros. But Villa was not laughing because he needed that blood."

"Poncho Villa was never in Reynoso," said Lopez.

The drink made the other ranchers bold and Francisco found their teasing a strain on his dignity—considering he owned the greatest bull in Sonora. Francisco put his fists on the bar and glared at Lopez.

"I never spoke to Poncho Villa and he probably never even saw me," Francisco said, "But by the Virgin and Jesus and all the saints I saw him. I only saw him once but I saw the bastard alright, just after cannons of the General Pershing blew up his headquarters and then the school."

"But why the blood of little boys?" asked Rolendez. He couldn't get over that part.

"It did not matter whose stinking blood it was," Francisco said, settling deeper into his chair. "It is just that us kids were the first people Villa's men rounded up because we could not fight back. His headquarters was in the church on the north side of town, and Pershing blew it to pieces and everyone in it, including seven of Villa's officers. Four of them were still alive but were busted up and bleeding to death so Villa's men rounded us up and took us to the schoolhouse. There was a doctor there and he told us this was our chance to help the revolution and give the country back to the people, back to us. There were about a dozen of us kids, two girls even, and we were all scared.The doctor said he needed only a little blood, and I got even more scared because I had never seen a needle before. They sat us in a line and strapped our arms to the table and told us not to move. The doctor started at the other end. When he put the needle into the first boy and I saw his blood flowing out the hose I got terrified and knew I was going to die. But the doctor told us all to relax and not move and that we did not have to worry because we had a lot of blood in our bodies and Villa did not need so much of it."

"I thought you said it was Villa's wounded men, not Villa who needed the little boys' blood," Moreno cracked.

"Fuck you Moreno, you black indio. I am telling you the truth and you know it is the truth because I never lie."

Lopez howled till the bottles shook on the counter top.

"I am not talking about what I tell my wife. I am talking about Poncho Villa, who needed our blood. And he got it." Francisco's face flushed red and trails of sweat streamed down his cheeks. "I was the last kid that devil doctor rigged up and it took three soldiers to hold me still. I knew I was dead and started screaming and pulling at the belts, but it was no good. I could only watch my blood flow out the tube. They kept those needles in there alright, until the first two kids had died, still strapped to the table, every last drop drained out of them. The girl next to me turned white and started getting drowsy, then I did too. I panicked and tried pulling the needle out with my teeth but a soldier grabbed my hair and pulled my head back. Then there was a big explosion."

Someone knocked a bottle off the bar and it shattered on the floor but Francisco didn't move. Nobody did.

"My ears rang," Francisco resumed, "and the room filled with smoke. When it cleared, a wall was missing and the doctor was dead and so were two of the soldiers. There was another soldier but when he got up and saw what had happened he ran off. I finally got the needle out of my arm with my teeth and chewed through the belt and got free. All the kids looked like ghosts and were dead except the girl next to me, and I think she died later. The tubes all emptied into these sacks and several had burst in the explosion. The floor was covered in blood and the place smelled like a slaughterhouse. Then I heard the horses and I went out through the open wall, and that's when I saw Villa."

"His cavalry was charging down the street and thundered right past me. Villa was up at the front, riding that big piebald. He was the only one wearing a military uniform, with a hat too small for him, and I saw him ride by."

Francisco took the rosary from me and stared at the piece of pot iron hanging on it.

"I realized my foot was burning so I picked up my foot and found this piece of metal under it. It came out of Pershing's cannon and had blown the schoolroom up. I tried to pick it up but it was still hot and it burned my fingers." Francisco's eyes were glassy and he pulled his hand over his sweaty face. Nobody said anything for a long time.

"That was somebody else in the military uniform, because Poncho Villa was never in Reynoso," López finally said.

"Then it was someone who looked like Poncho Villa," Rolendez suggested, talking through the lemon slice in his mouth.

"If you have ever seen a photo of Poncho Villa, you would know that nobody in Mexico looks anything like the bastard," Moreno said.

"Maybe Francisco did see him," de la Rubio suggested.

"You fool," Lopez said. "I told you my uncle—"

"You're uncle can't even read," Rolendez cut in.

"It's all a story, right out of the mescal bottle," said Moreno.

"Should of had Poncho looking for a virgin's blood," de la Rubio said. "Better for the story."

"There were no virgins in Reynoso back then," Lopez said. "And there still aren't." Lopez was from Estado Sinaloa.

"These Reynoso girls—they like the verga too much," laughed de la Rubio, also from Sinaloa.

"Who told you that?" Rolendez bristled.

"Your daughters," de la Rubio said.

Lopez roared and Rolendez jumped up and he and de la Rubio screamed and waved their fists at each other, but they were both over fifty and it was all show—though I didn't know it then. Francisco was still staring at the shard of metal in his palm. Then he closed his big brown fist over the piece of metal, lost in the distances of his mind.

All the way back to El Paso I asked Dad about Villa and the General Pershing and the shard of iron from his cannon and about Francisco Orozco's account. Finally Dad said, "It's all just a story, Carlos."

"A lie?"

"A story is a better word."

"Maybe it is true then," I said.

"Part of it is true, Carlos. It's just that Francisco is not old enough to have seen it himself."

"But Don Francisco looks very old. A hundred at least."

"At least," Dad said.

For years afterwards I thought that I would grow up to be a man like Don Francisco, who looked nothing like me and acted nothing like my father. Sometimes in a dream I would see Poncho Villa's men nailing my father to the door. Several times they buried me in the desert, up to my chin, and when I saw the horses galloping toward me I'd wake with a start.

Beneath the Glass Bubble

Searching for Salathea's grave was the kind of offbeat quest that suited Jeff Wills perfectly. Like most crack adventurers I've known, Jeff and society were barely on speaking terms. From certain angles he was twenty-eight, from others, fifty. His stormy face—his whole body, really—resembled a jagged limestone statue struck to life. This troubled some people; nobody felt comfortable before his restless eyes. And he was a mean bastard. Literally. He'd been pawned off at birth to a string of foster parents he'd never talk about. I was probably the only person who knew this, or that his natural father hailed from Riverside, a few miles away. At least Jeff thought he came from there, though I never knew how he found that out and never pressed him about it. I did know Jeff spent years trying to find him, but never could and finally gave up. The whole business drove him away from entangling relationships and straight down the Blue Nile in East Africa and the fuming Coruh in Turkey, historical first descents that both times killed his partners and cast a thundercloud over his calling and his life. Maybe it was because I was a couple years older, or had taken Jeff on his first Class 5 river—the Frazier, in Canada—but we got on well enough and always had.

Every Wednesday afternoon throughout one summer, a dozen of us would meet at the base of Mt. Rubidoux (hardly a mountain, just a swollen knoll a couple miles square and three-hundred feet high). Just west lies the Rubidoux Wash, a scrubby gray arroyo that for ten months a year teams with poison sumac and yellow jackets; but when July burns the snow off distant Mt. San Gregornio, a seasonal river, narrow and treacherous, tears through the wash at speed. During that one summer we must have paddled the twelve miles through the wash a dozen times. And every trip, to and from, we'd pass the little graveyard in Mt. Rubidoux's eastern shadow, with its rococo headstones and moldering statues, its little marble chambers girded by rusting chains.

One Wednesday, when the smog was like ink and the mercury pressed ninety, nobody showed but Jeff and me. He'd brought a six-pack of beer, so we skipped the paddling, sat in the lee of a boulder and popped a couple. We weren't four cans into it when Jeff asked if I knew about Salathé. I laughed. Somebody was always nudging the running joke along—that legendary Swiss explorer John Salathé was buried in the cemetery below. I don't know who started the ludicrous tale, but nobody believed it. When Jeff asked me if I absolutely knew it was bunk, I understood what he was getting at. We were out of beer and had nothing better to do.

For half an hour we wandered around the cemetery. I'd been in other bone yards before, but mostly your Forest Lawn variety—vast, shady grounds like billion-dollar golf courses, with towering "Roman" statues and enough cut flowers to make a man with a hangnail long to die. I wouldn't call the Rubidoux Memorial Cemetery a sacrilege to the dead, but the place hadn't seen a proper trimming in years, and much of the lawn resembled a wheat field, though rockier.

Most gravesites were from the middle of the last century, when anyone with money built the departed a little shrine. On the modest and forgotten headstones we read names like Sean O'Mally and Ricardo Vinicelli, first-generation Americans whose very bones were dust. One marble headstone, under a patina of lichen, read: "Timothy MacInnis A Scotsman 1869." The place seemed to have a voice to it, but it was so muted and long-ignored that I'd never make out the words until I too was host to the dead. We never even looked for John Salathé's grave.

Walking back to our cars, we passed over a parched section of crab grass, and Jeff suddenly tripped on a corner of gravestone. The mower and hose never reached this part of the yard. The coarse turf had completely overtaken dozens of little stone plots which, had Jeff not tripped on one, we would never have suspected were there. We pulled back the patch of grass and scraped the soil off the one-foot-square piece of slate Jeff had stumbled over. It read: "Dorothy Ann Reniky 1912-1932." I lingered over it, knowing it might have been fifty years since someone had noticed this woman's name.

I've never bothered tangling with impossible questions, but I could not help wondering who Dorothy Ann Reniky was, or had been, and what it meant to drop into the world, drift through twenty quick years and then fade under a shroud of crab grass. It didn't take much imagination to see my own name chiseled on that little square of stone.

We pulled the grass off a bunch of other graves as well, just to let the light play across the inscriptions. On several, there were little glass bubbles, cloudy and calcified, near the bottoms of the gravestones. Jeff took off his shirt and rubbed the raised glass of one grave, which grew more and more transparent. Begrudgingly, an old, very small portrait came slowly into focus. Not quickly enough for Jeff, however, who spit on the glass bubble and put all of himself into the work. In moments the glass cleared, and staring out at the world was a remarkably well-preserved photo of a boy, too young to talk, though his huge, bucolic smile spoke to us. The inscription said Miguel Domingo Santana had died in 1929, aged two. His giggle had been silent for sixty years, but now you could hear the echo.

We quickly located more gravestones that had portraits, and we set to polishing, feeling responsible for a resurrection of a kind. We'd peeled back the grass and the years and all kinds of folk were part of the continuum again. Jeff, meanwhile, had moved to the flanks, where several newer gravestones lay bare to the sun. One had a glass bubble. Jeff started buffing it clean. Suddenly, the shirt froze in Jeff's hand and his features set like the day of judgment, his eyes riveted on the small picture beneath the bubble. I joined him. The inscription said Milton H. Roth had died the previous year. A little figuring told us he'd been sixty-one. He must have died broke to get planted in that blighted patch of weeds. The photo was of a young and hale Milton Roth. The limestone face, the nervous eyes–Jeff might as well have been looking into a mirror.

First Time

November 12, 1958. Warren Harding, George Whitmore and Wayne Merry are lashed to a hanging stance 3,150 feet up El Capitan. The days are cold and short, and already afternoon shadows streak up the wall beneath them. They gaze overhead, and wonder: Will we ever get off? Will it ever be over?

On this, their final push, the trio has been on the wall eleven days, twice as long as any American has ever spent on a rock climb. Below in the shadows lies a tale of forty-five days spread over eighteen months, every day a pitched battle, every lead sieged. They've met obstacles no rock climber has ever seen, let alone mastered —wild pendulums, nailing expanding flakes thin as flapjacks, plus the back-breaking task of hauling vast supplies up the cliffside. And now, only a fifty-foot headwall bars them from the top of the mightiest rock wall in the contiguous United States. But that headwall, that last fifty feet, is dead blank and severely overhanging. They'll have to retreat 350 feet to Camp 6 and a good ledge, and tackle the headwall in the morning.

There comes a time in every great climber's career when technique or fitness or even genius falls short, when only brute willpower can close the deal. Harding considers his swollen hands, the mangled gear and frayed ropes, the rats that gnawed through haul bags, the rain and sleet and chilling retreats, his running feuds with rangers, the private terrors and sleepless nights and yet just now, hanging in a web of tattered slings, he can nearly spit to the top.

Warren Harding is not going down.

As darkness sets in, Harding starts bolting. And in an epic no climber should ever forget, he hammers through the night, finally punches home the twenty-eighth and last bolt, and stumbles to the top just as dawn spills into Yosemite Valley. The first ascent of The Nose, one of the greatest, and certainly the most-sought-after pure rock climb in the world, is a done thing.

◆ ◆ ◆

I had just started college when I first began spending summers in Yosemite Valley. By the time classes let out in June, the valley was scalding and most American climbers had migrated fifty miles north to Tuolumne Meadows, where the climbing was good and the days cool. But the valley had the famous climbs, the big climbs, so I stayed there, often tying in with Europeans who welcomed the heat and the long Yosemite routes.

During my second summer there, I teamed up with British ace Ron Fawcet, who was probably the finest free climber in Europe, and would be for a decade to come. My age (nineteen), he too was principally a crag climber looking to extend his repertoire. We'd been climbing together for some weeks, doing short, hard free climbs, and feeling pretty good about ourselves; but every time we passed El Cap, we'd glance at each other like thieves because the amplitude of that rock, and the towering challenge it presented, totally overshadowed the silly little routes we were bagging.

So long as we pursued the dream, we felt we were dangling on the lip of heroism; but we were doing neither on the short routes. The dream was not a 150-feet high. It was a mile high and profoundly dramatic. The short routes were exciting, but excitement was a poor substitute for the theater of doom found on the big walls—and we both knew it.

One day at Arch Rock, we were both lacing up for a grim route that was barely a rope-length long. I looked up at it, started laughing and said, "What are we doing cocking around on this pissant climb?" The shorties all at once seemed like a game of charades, a surrogate ritual for our rendezvous with the dream. There was no more putting it off.

The next day we climbed a long route on Middle Cathedral Rock—or started to. We gained a big ledge after a couple hundred feet, and spent the rest of the day looking across at El Cap—just opposite—eyeballing the various routes and talking about trying it "one day."

This was tricky business, working on the fringe of the Big Question: When do we go for it? Physically, we knew we could do it. But pondering that mammoth chunk of granite it's your mind, not your body, that shudders. We intently listened to each other's voice, studied each other's eyes, trying to reckon without asking how the other guy truly felt about it. It's a known fact that you can't look at El Capitan and lie at the same time, not about wanting to climb it anyway. So we didn't press each other, afraid the other guy might be on shaky ground and try to lie, or start mumbling excuses about why he didn't want to climb it when you knew damn well he did. He had to, or he was a coward and an outright fraud. By the end of that day on Middle Cathedral, the Big Question had grown and swollen between us like a great festering boil. We'd have to lance it with the Big Answer if we wanted to continue as partners.

"Maybe we should have a go at it," Ron finally offered.

"Before it grows any more," I said.

There is a ritual all climbers perform before a long climb, and it hasn't changed much since "gentleman mountaineers" plowed up Mt. Blanc in tweeds and hob-nailed boots two hundred years ago. The ritual flows from the fact that the quicker you get through the formalities and onto the route, the less chance you have of changing your mind; and after hauling Harding's epic through my brain a thousand times, I wanted to put that all aside and get on with it. Big climbs are not casual business, not something done for the fun of it, and there are always ready reasons why not to go. So when the urge strikes, you move on it.

The ritual goes like this: First, you pick the route, then a partner. Then you both go down with binoculars and study the climb. A wall veteran can tell much by a good glassing; a rookie can only get scared. The devil may show you a little flea of a man on your route, half a mile up, floundering and flailing and hardly moving at all. You picture yourself in his boots, glance at your partner, and go to the bar to drown the urge—if anything's left of it. If the urge is still kicking, you return to camp, spread a tarp out and, referring to the guidebook and any tips you've picked up from friends or acquaintances who've climbed the route, you set about organizing the mountain of gear.

Dozens of pitons are lined up side by side, according to size. Nuts are arranged, carabiners linked and counted dozens of times, slings tied and retied, ropes inspected, water bottles taped and filled. Then you stand back and stare at the gear. Then you stare at your partner. Then you go back and stare at the route some more. If you can still look your partner in the eye, you'll probably go through with it, return to camp, pack all the gear and the food into the haul bag and try to knock off early. And anybody who says he slept well, or at all, before that first big climb is either crazy or a liar.

We slithered out of our sleeping bags around four-thirty in the morning, and hiked to the base in the dark. The waiting before a big climb is harsh, but hiking to the cliff is the worst part of all. A few climbers are loud and won't stop yakking because the worm is turning hard and deep and their balls are up in their throats. Most are stone-faced and sweating the big drop. But the cliff, once gained, which you vicariously know so well, eases the stress and loneliness of the march. We started up at first light, hoping to get far up the wall that first day. The normal time needed to ascend the Nose was three to four days; we brought food and water for a day and a half.

From the start, Ron and I climbed like madmen, trying to quickly get ourselves so irreversibly committed we couldn't retreat, so the only way off was up. Up to that day, my typical climbing outing involved driving out to Suicide Rock or Joshua Tree National Monument, cranking off a couple gymnastic, picayune routes, then retiring to McDonald's for burgers and enormous talk. But El Cap was commitment with a capital C, and like most newcomers to the high crag, part of me kept yelling: "Get the hell off this while you still can." It was simple inexperience talking. And it didn't help that the ground kept getting farther away, but the summit didn't seem to get one inch closer—an optical illusion particular to all big climbs. The secret is to stay focused on the physical climbing. If you simply cannot manage the climbing and exhaust yourself trying, fair enough. An honest failure never haunts you because the body knows no shame. But if you let your mind defeat you, if you bail off because the "vibes" are weird and you let fear run away with itself, you have not truly failed, rather defaulted, and it will nag you like a tune till your dying day—or until you return and set things straight.

At the 600-foot mark we gained the first big pendulum—a wild running swing right to the "Stoveleg Crack" (so named because on the first ascent, Harding nailed it using four crude pitons forged from the legs of an old stove scavenged from the Berkeley city dump). From the top of a long bolt ladder, you lower down about sixty feet, then start swinging back and forth. Now at speed, you go for it, feet kicking hard, digging right. You hurtle a corner, and as you feel the momentum ebbing, you dive. If you've chanced it right, you plop a hand into a perfect jam just as your legs start to swing back. You kip your torso, kick a boot in and you're on line. A laser-cut fracture shoots up the prow for 350 feet of primarily perfect hand-jamming, the wall as smooth as a bottle and not a ledge in sight, each lead ending in stark, hanging belays. The climbing went quickly and by noon, we were on El Cap Towers, a perfectly flat granite patio about twenty-by-six feet.

This was our first chance to catch our breath and take stock of our situation, racing as we'd been just to get there. I peered up and across and straight down, and images were thrown back that no climber can entirely fathom and no one in any language can do justice. "Holy fucking mackerel!" I yelled. What a strange mingling of terror and exhilaration I felt gazing down at the miniature busses and cars creeping over a world we'd left only a few hours before, but from which we were now separated by a distance that could not be measured by any yardstick. I flashed on my friends in Camp 4, half of them foreigners, and marveled how the dream extended beyond local or even national interests, and how much more outrageous the deed was from the idea of it. If it entailed physical dangers, I reasoned, surely they were worth facing. But there was no explaining away the shocking uneasiness of facing the distance to our goal.

Above the comparatively low-angled Stovelegs, the upper wall rifles up into perfect corners—like a cut melon. To our right looms the fearsome sweep of the southwest face, which at dawn draws fabulous hues into its keeping. There lie the world's most notorious big-wall climbs, and it's hard to imagine an arena where man has fewer claims and less authority. We were following a good, secure crack system, but no such thing lay to our right. No ledges, no ramps. Nothing but a chilling, ninety-five-degree wall, a shadowy void damn scary to even look at. Since Royal Robbins, Chuck Pratt, Tom Frost and Yvon Chouinard first scaled it in 1964, via the North America Wall, a dozen other routes had been established thereon; and what epics this great sprawl of granite must have witnessed. From our ledge on El Cap Towers, it seemed we could hear the echoes of all the tense leaders who had once passed there—their terrors and doubts, hooking and bashing their way up the wall's overhanging immensity. And it seemed, too, that we could see their moon eyes glaring at belay bolts hanging half out of the gritty diorite bands, where a dropped piton strikes nothing but the ground half a mile below. A precious few specialists thrive on this kind of work, and they make the most curious study in all rock climbing.

We pushed on, traversing up and across the Gray Band, a nebulous stretch at mid-height that follows an intrusion of flaky ash monzonite. By early afternoon we'd reached Camp Four, a small recess of puny terraces below the final corner, which soared straight to the top, 1,200 feet above. Suddenly, the breeze died, and the cruel heat welling off the white rock stopped us dead. The next ledge was 500 feet higher, so we decided to bivouac right there, on Camp 4.

No longer absorbed with hauling bags and climbing hard and fast, the bivy was like suddenly finding ourselves becalmed after a typhoon. We dropped anchor, clasped the rigging, gaped up and down and every which way, trying to get our bearings. We studied the topo map to reckon where we were, and what lay between us and the home port on top. We tossed off some small talk, sipped the precious water, nibbled sardines and cheese and tried to ignore the fact we were marooned on a knobby, down-sloping ledge scarcely big enough to sit on, 2,100 feet up the side of a cliff, with 1,200 feet of heavy weather overhead. Exhausted, we eventually laid back and tried to settle in, rattled by the naked feelings dancing through our heads.

If wall climbing is good for nothing else, it's a sure way to find out, once and for all, how you really feel—not what you're expected to feel, or have been told or taught to feel. Slowly, you take on the stark, naked aspect of the great wall, and sink into the tide pools of your mind. It's weird and disturbing to see what's prowling around there, and you can't surface no matter how hard you try. Down you go, into the silences within yourself. Finally, you hit bottom and just hover there, weightless, face to face with those ancient fears and feral sensations that reach back to when man first slithered from the ooze, reared up on his hind legs and bolted for the nearest cave to steady up. It's very much like being insane, but far more intense because you're so aware of it. Mastering these feelings, the inner tension of being strung taut between fear and desire, is the fundamental challenge for the wall climber.

It is one thing to simply battle your way up a wall, jaw clenched, heart thumping like a paddle wheel. But to thrive up there, to dominate the climbing with confidence, to feel like you belong, requires a transformation of character hard to accept for a young climber. Up there with Ron on my first El Cap bivy, it seemed strangely unfair to have to grow all the way up at nineteen. I refused (in fact, passed out from weariness), then woke with a start at the emptiest hour of the night, completely disoriented. I writhed a bit, and came taut to the rope with a jerk. My shoulders and head flopped over the ledge and I might as well have been peering over the edge of the world. Mother of God!

Ron, sitting bolt up right beside me, said, "We're in trouble, big bloody trouble." Only then did I realize just how high we fools had flown. Then Ron started laughing and when I looked over at him, with his gravedigger's grin, I realized I wasn't looking at a young tough from Sheffield anymore. And all the tension we'd hauled up there suddenly vanished. I sat awake for a moment longer, voluptuous with fatigue, then fell back and slept the sleep of the dead.

By mid-morning the next day we were well into the upper corners, more than 2,500 feet up the wall and into the really prime terrain. And loving it despite the lines getting snagged, our feet aching from standing in slings, the grime and grit and aluminum oxide from the carabiners stinging our hands, the flesh barked and torn, shoulders aching from thirty-pound slings of nuts and fifty carabiners. Our throats were raw, teeth gummed, lips cracked, tongues like rawhide because you can never bring enough water, neck and arms flame red, backs crooked from hauling the bag, clothes spangled with sardine oil and sweat-soaked from sun to fry eggs by. But we didn't care because we were on El Capitan.

From the start, all the way up to the bivouac, I found myself measuring my reasons for confidence against the towering danger I was in, most of it imagined. But now I had gotten above all measuring, and my mind had taken a back seat to savor the chase as my body frantically went about its work. Nearing the top, the exposure is so enormous, and your perspective so distorted, that the horizontal world becomes incomprehensible. You're a granite astronaut, dangling in a kind of space/time warp, and the exhilaration is superb. Men talk of dreaming Gardens of Eden and cities of gold, but nothing can touch being pasted way up in the sky like that. It is a unique drama for which no tickets are sold.

Other routes are steeper, more exposed than The Nose. But no route has a more dramatic climax. The Harding headwall is short—fifty overhanging feet—and after a few friction steps, you're suddenly on level ground. But since Harding's day, some maniac had re-engineered the last belay so that it hung at the very brink of the headwall, where all thirty-five pitches spill down beneath your boots. It's a master stroke, that hanging belay, for it gives climbers a moment's pause at one of the most spectacular spots in all of American climbing. Cars creep along the valley's loop road three-quarters of a mile below, broad forests appear as brushed green carpets and, for one immortal moment, you feel like a giant in a world of ants. Then suddenly, it's over.

But it wasn't over. Ron had scrambled to the top, had hauled the bag and was yelling for me to hustle so we could get on with our lives. But I didn't move. I couldn't move. I kicked back in my stirrups and looked around. I didn't know why. I had never lingered before, always pressing on with gritted teeth, surging, fighting both myself and the climb to gain the top. Suddenly I was free of all that, of all the incessant rushing; so I just hung there and took it all in, and for the first time in my climbing career I seemed to fully appreciate what I was doing, how outrageous it was. Only by lingering did I get past all the sweat and vistas and paranoia and flashes of bliss, and only then did the whole disparate experience harmonize itself into a point of emotional symmetry and purpose.

The moment lasted about a minute. Without knowing it, I'd been chasing that moment since the first time I'd laced up climbing shoes. Yet even then, I couldn't really recognize the tune. (Some years later I was browsing through Bruce Chatwin's notes at the end of his book *Dreamtime*, and ran across the following paragraph: "A white explorer in Africa, anxious to press ahead with his journey, paid his porters for a series of forced marches. But they, almost within reach of their destination, set down their bundles and refused to budge. No amount of extra payment would convince them otherwise. They said they had to wait for their souls to catch up.")

Those first few moments on horizontal ground are so disorienting they hurl you into a transitional spin where little registers. A big wall is strong drink for a young mind. Few can handle it neat; most are hungover for hours, even days. Whether you've taken one day or one week, you are a different person than the one who started 3,000 feet below. I've heard of climbers hugging boulders, punching partners and weeping openly—some from relief, some sad that it was over. I've seen other climbers babbling incoherently, and I once saw a middle-aged Swiss team simply shake hands, abandon every stitch of their gear—ropes, rack, haul bags, the works—and stroll off for the trail down, their climbing careers made and finished right there. Ron and I only remember coiling ropes and bolted for the East Ledges descent route.

We got back down to the loop road about two that afternoon, exhausted by the nervous depression which always follows a wall. As we stumbled around a bend, El Capitan came into view, backlit and burning at the edges. For all the raw labor and anxieties of the climb, it was natural that, all the way up, I should wonder if I was committing more to a venture than it was actually worth, if I was putting too much into too little. But if there is anything of a magnitude that can blow a person off his feet, it's that first ground-level view of a wall he's just climbed. Too little? The second we saw it, Ron and I stood in the middle of the road and gaped up at it with our mouths open. It looked about ten miles high. And how long ago it seemed we'd been up there, and how strange, as though we'd seen it in a movie, or in a dream, and had suddenly awakened, half remembering what it was we dreamed.

My Friend Phil

For the half dozen years before Paraguay's Rio Cayman swept him away from us (along with his two kayaking partners, Marty Silver and Rick Navarro), the adventure community was divided into two camps: those who had been with Davenport, and those who had not. Philip and I had been together and in trouble years before the world had ever heard of Philip Randolph Davenport.

The Davenport family was from another planet, or so thought my father, Woody, an Aspen carpenter who had built the deck on the Davenports' summer home near Ajax Mountain. The home, a palatial article set on a hillside overlooking Golden Butte, was a bizarre amalgam of Manhattan chic and aboriginal Peru, and suggested the eccentric union of the Davenports themselves.

Herbert Davenport was a kook gentleman anthropologist who had spent nearly twenty years studying antique cultures deep in the Peruvian rain forest. Katherine Putnam Davenport was a bejeweled, vinegary former debutante with a tongue like a carving knife. She was the kind that didn't go out in the sun without an umbrella. Her husband had been so long out of circulation that when he returned to the states from the jungle, he was unfit, if not incapable, of any legitimate work. Katherine's tacit agreement with Davenport patriarchs was that so long as she kept her husband on the sidelines, where he couldn't embarrass anyone, their ration of the enormous family fortune was secure.

For nearly a dozen years Katherine and Herbert had seen one another only at Christmas and for a few weeks each summer.

When phlebitis finally drove Herbert from the rainforest for good (along with Philip, who had spent most of his childhood with his father in Peru), he and Katherine were like strangers thrown together. But Herbert was lost in the civilized world without his wife's direction, and she was hopeless without his money. For the first year they tolerated each other in a curious, aristocratic kind of way. After another year they were an inseparable odd couple.

The Davenports spent their summer months in Aspen, where Philip and I had both been in my Dad's Explorer Scout troop and fell in together. When the Davenports invited me to join them for a week near La Paz, Baja California, Dad thought it a wise plan, since I was nearly sixteen and had never left Colorado. Philip was rather wild, and his folks were from Mars, but they were respectable and moneyed, and, if anything should happen, Dad figured they could get me back to Aspen quickly enough.

The Davenport casita belonged to Herbert's brother, Harold, who had spent a bundle trimming it out, and used it once every couple of years or not at all. A couple hundred yards below the paved road leading to La Paz, and close by the sea, lay a hard-packed dirt road crowded with dog carts, kids on rusty bicycles, women with black rebozos pulled over their shoulders, dragging wailing ninos by the hand, and peons with great loads of fire-wood on their bare shoulders, trudging toward the charcoal fac-tory in town. Just off this dirt road, set back in a copse of green bamboo, was the casita—a diamond in the rough if ever I saw one.

Set up on creaky oak pylons, the three-bedroom house cantilevered over gulf waters famous for sport fishing. The exte-rior was plain, but the interior was tooled out for proto-Mexican gentry, with portraits of Cantinflas and Pedro Infante and a few San Sebastian bullfighters on the reed walls; silver-trimmed wicker furniture covered with combed hides on the wooden floor; and a collection of priceless Spanish glassware and Toltec artifacts in filigreed cabinets against the den walls. A silver horseshoe hung over the kitchen door for suerte, or luck.

Katherine Davenport hated the place the minute she got there. Never mind the decor: ruffians prowled the dirt road just out the front door, the electricity was off and on, mostly off, the humidity was terminal, and the flooring was warped in spots and she could see the anxious ocean through the gaps.

On the second night, when Phil and I were swinging face down in hammocks and trying to spit through rifts in the floor, Mrs. Davenport let out a scream that was heard in Panama. A cucuracha the size of a taquito had scampered across her bedspread, and several fiddler crabs had made their way into the bedroom as well. She swore she wouldn't stay in that house one second longer. Pop Davenport loaded up the rental Jeep and took his wife to the Hotel Hidalgo, a five-star lodging in town. We could come if we wanted to. We didn't. Pop Davenport would swing by in the morning to take us out for breakfast. The Jeep wheeled off, and we were alone.

Philip rifled the liquor cabinet and came away with a bottle of Jose Cuervo Gold. We moved to the back of the house and a warped plank staircase—barely eight feet wide and set between two rotting pylons—that spilled from the den straight into the sea, where a small, flimsy dinghy was tethered. We sat on the last step with our legs in salt water and gazed out over the moon-rinsed gulf, talking about climbing the Maroon Bells back in Aspen, and maybe doing some bull riding here in La Paz—if we could find a bull. The tequila clobbered us, burning all the way down to our toes.

The bottle was only a quarter gone when we spotted a giant cutlass carving through the water, flashing like mother-of-pearl as it swiveled into the moonlight. "Shark" Philip whispered.

I bounded up a couple stairs to a pylon as Philip jumped into the dinghy, snatched an oar and started bashing the water.

"Frenzied movements attract them," Philip cried, beating away. "I read it in *Argosy*."

"Attracts them?" I yelled, clinging to the pylon. "Jesus, Phil. That fin's big as a STOP sign. You sure you wanna be fuckin' with it?" Phil thrashed the water even harder. I moved to the top step as the fin swept close by the dinghy, circled under the house and sliced back into the deep. Philip jumped from the dinghy, splashed up the stairs and into the house, then returned with the remains of our chicken dinner, chumming the water with bones and chicken necks and gizzards. Several times the gleaming fin cruised past but never as close as the first time.

"Blood," Philip said angrily, "We need blood." And he hurled the tequila bottle into the sea.

It was nearly dawn before I could knock off in my hammock, picturing that great fin circling under the bedroom floor. When I woke the next morning I found Philip in the kitchen, studying the big silver horseshoe hanging above the door. Pop Davenport had already come and gone, and Philip showed me a thick wad of peso notes to prove it. His mom had a fever and his father didn't want to leave her alone in the hotel. We would have to fetch our own breakfast.

Philip reached up above the door jamb and yanked the big silver horseshoe free from its nails, his eyes burning. "We're going fishing, Jim."

We jogged up to the main road, hailed an autobus and were soon scudding around central La Paz, grabbing a cocktail de camarones in one stall, ogling the senoritas in others. We moved on to have an old man, hunched over a foot-powered grinder, mill one end of the silver horseshoe into a pick, sharp as fate. I watched the fury of peso notes changing hands, Philip rattling off espanol like a native. Smoking lung-busting Delicados, sin filtros, we hustled on through the fish market, ankle deep in mullet offal. At another stall a fleshy woman, her cavernous cleavage dusted with talc, cut ten feet of thick chain link off a gigantic, rusty spool. "For leader," said Philip, grabbing my arm and racing off. From another lady in a booth hung with crocheted murals of Jesus Christo, Philip bought 200 yards of 500-kilo test polypropylene rope. Meanwhile, her husband welded the chain link leader onto the sharpened horseshoe, sparks from the acetylene rig raining over Jesus like shooting stars.

"Now for the bait."

We took a cab to the slaughterhouse on the edge of town. Outside the reeking, sheet-metal structure, Philip waved through a curtain of flies and stopped an Indian girl, maybe sixteen. Her hair was pulled back in thick black braids to bare a face so striking that armadillos raced up my spine just looking at her. She was selling fried pork rinds and sweet bread, and when Philip asked her a probing question, she killed him with her eyes. Philip talked some more, cajoling her. I understood nothing of their machine-gun Spanish. Slowly, the girl's glare melted into a snigger. When Phil's hand went out with a ten-peso note, she reached for it quick as a frog's tongue. But not quick enough. Philip shook his head, flashing a wily smile and holding the bill out of reach. She answered his smile with a sly one of her own, glanced around at empty streets, then quickly hiked up her white muslin blouse and for about one thousandth of a second my eyes feasted on two perfect brown globes crowned with two perky, pinto bean-like nipples. Then her shirt was back down and the bill was gone from Philip's hand and she was two golden heels hot-footing to some shady nook to admire the gringo boy's money.

"I'd marry her in a second," Phil said, "If I was old enough."

We took a bus back to the casita, laden with a giant bull's heart wrapped in brown paper and twine and a bucket of red slop so heavy it put my hand to sleep.

On the stairs behind the house Phil baited the sharpened horseshoe with the ruby-colored bull's heart, duct-taped a soccer ball to the chain-link leader just below where he'd tied on the polypropylene rope, then neatly coiled the rope on the stairs and lashed the free end round one of the creaky pylons. As he hefted the bucket of sloppy entrails into the small dinghy, my balls shriveled to the merest garbanzos.

"You can either watch the line here in the bow, or row. You pick."

"I thought we were going to just chuck the thing in from here," I said.

"Shark won't go for it. You saw how he shied away last night. And anyway, I bought all this rope."

Two hundred yards of new rope seemed a poor excuse to row into shark-infested waters in a leaky dinghy full of blood and guts; but Phil was already in the boat yelling, "Come on, Jim. It's a two-minute job."

I took the oars and rowed straight out into the gulf, my limbs trembling so horribly I could barely pull water. The dinghy was overloaded and tippy as hell and several geysers spewed up through cracks in the flexing hull. I watched the casita grow smaller, the line slithering out from its coil. My chest heaved. The water quickly rose around my tennis shoes.

Fifty yards out, Phil tossed the bucket of gore overboard and a dull red ring bled out around us.

"That sucker's any closer than Acapulco, he'll smell this," he said. "Believe it."

"I do."

Phil chucked the big ruby heart overboard with a plunk, the weight yanking out the chain leader which chattered over the low gunnel of the dinghy. The soccer ball shot out, and sank. Phil panned the flat blue plane for a moment. Then the soccer ball suddenly popped up near us, the waters boiled and he screamed, "Put your back into it Jim, or we're goners!"

I heaved at the oars, my heart thundering in my ears and my lungs gasping down mouthfuls of air, the dinghy fairly hydroplaning, Phil bailing furiously with the bucket and screaming, "Pull, man, pull." I pulled harder and faster, trying to retrace the polypropylene line floating on the water, marking the way back home. The flimsy oars bent horribly as Phil screamed to go faster and faster till my oars were driving like bee's wings. Twenty yards from the house we were both screaming, breathless and terrified, the dinghy shin-deep and sinking by the second. A final heave, and I powered right into the stairs: the dinghy buckled and split in half, dumping us into carnivorous waters. We splashed and groped for the stairs, then stampeded over each other and through the house and out the front door, puking salt water and howling, finally collapsing in the dirt in front of a man selling shaved ice from a push cart.

Phil lay in the dirt, breathing hard and feigning palsy, his face screwed up and his eyes rolled back in his head. My knees were clacking out loud and I started laughing so fearfully and so hard I couldn't stand and sort of collapsed into the dirt.

"Not that we're afraid to die or anything," Phil gasped.

The man with the pushcart couldn't have looked more confused if he'd seen a toro prance by on its hind legs.

After a few minutes we stole back into the house, tiptoeing a step at a time through the hall, through the narrow den, past the wall of glassware and artifacts, pausing at the open door and the stairs below and staring out over the gulf waters at the line sleeping on the surface and the soccer ball bobbing peacefully fifty yards away. There wasn't so much as a crawfish on the line. Never had been.

"Chickenshit shark," Phil mumbled. And we sat down.

For several hours we sat hip to hip on the stairs, gazing out at the bobbing soccer ball so hard that the flat horizon and the heat of high noon put us in a trance. Then everything was quiet. Too quiet.

"Wonder where the gulls went?" I asked, dizzy with tension.

The rope suddenly jumped out of the water, the staircase groaned and splinters flew off the pylon as the line lashed itself taut as a bowstring.

"He's hooked!" cried Phil.

We leaped up and grabbed the rope as the old pylon bowed against the stairs, rusty nails sprang up from fractured planks and sand crabs scurried out from dark places. Far out on the water we saw an invincible fin, a mad roil of water and a jagged snap. A scythe-shaped tail curled on itself and the rope went slack against the pylon. A gathering surge was tearing straight toward us, looking like a submarine surfacing as the line doubled back on itself. Twenty yards out, the fin swerved suddenly and headed out to open sea. We couldn't appreciate the monster's speed till we noticed the loose line, straightening fast as if it were lashed to a cigarette boat.

"Grab the rope, or the house is going with him," Phil yelled, lunging for the line.

There was no checking the creature, but I stupidly grabbed the rope anyway. The shark hit the slack line, wrenched me straight off the stairs and into the playground of the blazing gray terror. I barked knees and elbows furiously crabbing from the water and up the stairs, and I didn't stop running till the den. And there I stood, bloody and wheezing, dripping salt water onto a 19th-century Malagan rug. I was dry before I staggered back to the stairs.

The line was slack, then taut. Then slack again. We pulled. Phil cussed like a sailor. The rope smoked through my raw hands. I wanted to cry. We pulled some more.

After an hour, we'd gained a little. With the rope doubled round a pylon, there was just enough friction that we could lock the beast off—even gain some rope when the tension eased for a second. After two hours we'd reeled the creature a quarter of the way in. Several times it broke surface, obsidian eyes glinting in the sun. The line under my hands dripped red, and the salt water tortured the grooves seared into my palms. The more line we gained, the fiercer the combat. The monster would relax for a moment and we'd win a yard, then the line would twang tight, the pylon would pop and the remaining stairs would shudder under our bicycling feet. It was a standoff.

"We need help," Phil said. "Lock him off for a minute."

I braced against the pylon and held fast as the house behind me filled with dark-haired boys, street urchins in rags, and even the man with the push cart, snagged from the dirt road just out-side. When the line went momentarily slack, Philip unwound it from the pylon and, racing against time, ran the rope in a straight line from the water up the stairs and through the den, down the hall and right out the front door. The brown crowd turned its back on the casita, each man and boy clasping the rope over his shoulder, Philip yelling, "Hale. Hale, hooooooombres." The tug-of-war was on, "tiburon, tiburon grandote" yelled over and over like a chant at a futbol match.

Philip joined me on the crumbling stairs, hauling hand over hand now, the whole gulf one huge swell coursing toward us, quickly becoming a shark big as a four-man bobsled, thrashing against the straining rope.

"Let off," I yelled, releasing the line and backpedaling away, "Tell them to let off."

But it was no good. The gathering crowd was fifty feet past the front door, their feet churning the dust. Phil and I jumped to the pylon when, with one titanic lurch, they hauled the opalescent monster to light. Another heave, and it flopped bodylong onto the buckling stairs, the silver horseshoe hooked deep through its toothy lower jaw, the line taut as a guywire. The beast did a move from the deep, lurched a yard straight up off the stairs and, now airborne, was yanked right past us. Its bear-trap maw snapped and a sandpaper flank rasped the skin off my arm as he jackknifed over the stairs, through the open backdoor and into the den, a place of leisure and filigreed cabinets, of rum toddies and ripe mangos, of drowsy vacation afternoons. Another move from ten fathoms and he clipped the legs out from under the rosewood-and-ivory table.

"Let off, for Christ's sake," I screamed from the stairs. "Let it go."

But every man for five miles along the dirt road had latched onto that rope, and all fifty of them were hauling for pride and country: cabbies, rummies, compesinos, wood cutters, men in white suits and wraparound shades, a priest in huaraches (who looked exactly like Father Sera), and nine Guardia Nationales, yelling commands and tapping slackers with batons. But 900 pounds of tiger shark wasn't going easily. A smashing tail and the cabinets were gone, the Toltec artifacts were so many shards, the Spanish glassware, sand. Colossal teeth shreaded filigreed wood, ripped the hides off wicker chairs. A flip and a twirl and he unraveled the Malagan rug. The heaving crown pulled the monster further through the narrow den. Rich purple blood splattered over bright white walls. A deep-water kip, an airborne nosebutt—and a wall caved in. Salt-rotted wood fractured and floor slats snapped to attention as the ceiling dropped a yard and parted to show a splintered smile of blue Mexican sky.

And the brown mob pulled. The great monster died ten times, then lurched back to life, marking its passage through the open house by knocking sheetrock off the hallway walls, murdering grandfather clock, blasting the front door off its hinges.

At last the creature lay outside, its hornblende eyes on infinity, its jagged mouth open. One of the National Guardsman probed the cavity with his baton, and in a final show of sea force, the huge mouth snapped shut. The guardsman jumped back with a hickory stub in his hand, yelling, "Hijo de puta."

For nearly an hour we all stood around in a daze, staring at the great monster as kids prodded it with long sticks and several policeman posed for pictures taken with an antique Kodak Brownie camera Philip swore had no film in it.

Word of the conquest spread down the dirt road like a whirlwind, and shortly, a flatbed truck from the fish market sputtered up. Ten men log-rolled the beast onto the lift and then into the bed of the truck. In five more minutes the shark was a relic of memory. The crowd slowly went their way, thumping each other's back, and we were once again alone.

I was grated raw, rope-burned, sunburned, splintered, bloodied and spent, my trunks and shirt in tatters, one tennis shoe gone, my hands two oozing, pulpy knobs. Philip was completely unmarked. His shirt was still tucked in. But the casita couldn't have been more trashed had we trapped a grizzly inside it for two weeks—without food or water.

We tried a hundred different lies on each other but couldn't concoct an excuse as big as that shark. Finally, Philip went to the Hotel Hidalgo to try to explain; and in an example of his transcendental luck, he found his parents preparing to leave on the next plane for the states. His mother felt another night in Mexico might kill her. Without reservations, they were able to secure only two seats on the 3:30 p.m. Air Mexicana flight to Los Angeles; but Pop Davenport had booked us on the 6:50 flight that same night. The Davenports would wait for us at the airport in Los Angeles, and we'd all go to Disneyland.

Philip raced back to the casita and, after wandering through the ruins, said, "We've got to torch it."

"Torch it?"

"Yeah, burn it down."

I pictured myself in a Mexican jail. Forever.

"You want to try and explain this?" Philip laughed, glancing at the sea through a ten foot hole in the floor, then up through the widening hole in the roof. "This joint's dusted."

"How do we explain the fire?" I asked.

"We don't," Philip smiled. "That's the beauty of it. It burns down after we're gone. And it will."

Philip shagged into town, returned with a cab, a gallon of kerosene, and two votive candles. We threw our suitcases into the cab waiting on the dirt road, then Philip soaked the den floor with the kerosine, planted two candles in the middle of the buckled floor, lit them, walked out the open door and into the cab, and we were off.

As Air Mexicana flight 496 ground up off the tarmac, we spotted a plume of black smoke out east, rising off the fringe of the sea. Philip leaned back in his seat and said, "Wonder how long that sucker was?"

When Harold Davenport returned to Mexico two years later, he found two shrimp boats tied up to pylons where his vacation home had once stood. Nobody seemed to know how the fire had started. Or even when.

Last Place on No Map

(from Cerro Verde)

T he jet swept over the mighty Amazon just below its confluence with the Rio Negro, and Paul stared curiously at
the black and copper waters flowing side by side, as if separated by an invisible wall impermeable and arrow straight. A riff
of Portuguese came over the intercom–a queer, oily language
sounding like Spanish pronounced so miserably that Paul could
barely understand they were landing in Porto Velho in five minutes. The jet turned south, and began its descent.

He peered out the window again, and the landscape suddenly
changed. Below lay a hazy checkerboard–this square, a dwindling tract of pristine forest; that square, a raging fire; this
square, a vile scar, twenty miles across, spangled with thousands
upon thousands of splintered stumps. Thin, mud-red arteries
crisscrossed the smoldering chaos, a long queue of overloaded
logging trucks barreling along them. Paul leaned back in his seat
and sighed.

On the outskirts of Porto Velho, the cab sputtered along the
fringe of a tumbledown airport. A nonstop loop of battered
Beechcraft Twins–"air taxis"–landed on the pocked runway, dis-
gorged men huge with mud, boarded a dozen more, gassed up
and winged back to the interior. At strip's end, on the edge of a
fetid grey swamp, Paul found the four-walled MAF hangar and its
portentous sign: "Privativo." He handed the cabby a 1,000
cruzeiro note, and made for the hangar.

Inside, a lone pilot worked on the cylinder head of a STAL
Cessna. A lank edgy man of about thirty, he didn't look up as

Paul set his duffel down and walked over. The rain had thinned to an annoying mist.

"Hello," Paul said in English.

The pilot glanced up from the engine. "We don't run a charter service, if that's what you're looking for." He wore a Michigan State sweatshirt shot with holes, stained with avgas and Perma-Gasket.

"Someone here used to forward the mail for a friend of mine," Paul said.

"We forward a lot of mail."

"His name is Doctor Orlando Zavalla."

The pilot jerked his head from the engine well, shot Paul a look and said, "We don't go to Cerro Verde anymore."

"What about Doctor Zavalla?"

"Read my lips: We don't go to Cerro Verde." He turned his back and returned to the engine.

Paul grabbed the pilot's arm, gently pulled him around and said, "You wouldn't answer the letters, but I won't be ignored in person."

"Are you threatening me?"

"I'm asking you—about Dr. Zavalla."

"And I'm telling you, we haven't been to Cerro Verde in over a year. Now pardon me. I've got work."

Paul knew the type. And the attitude. At least half of them had it. The more backwater the post, the stranger these people were, or became.

"How do I get to Cerro Verde?"

"You don't. Goodbye."

Creed-bound and creed-mad, as his pride was fanatical, so would his wrath be uncontainable—if only Paul could pull his trigger point. He gambled, said, "Watch me," and picked up his duffel.

The pilot wheeled toward Paul. "You have no right to go there. The Methodist Foreign Legion built the mission in Cerro

Verde. It's our concern, not yours, not Doctor Orlando Zavalla's."

"Maybe your legion was a little too foreign for the locals," Paul said.

The pilot glared bitterly and said, "That mission had been there for twenty years, until Doctor Zavalla arrived."

"So he's still there?" Paul said.

"He took advantage of the situation," the pilot said, his face flushed and rancorous. "If he didn't cause it himself. He's nothing but an arrogant meddler, your doctor."

"Would you care for a cup of tea?"

Paul turned toward the new voice and a wan, painfully pious-looking woman. Roughly the pilot's age, her face was uncanny, eerie. Paul glanced back at the pilot, who had already returned to the engine, then back to the woman. Her honed green eyes were selfless. Paul said, "Yes. I could use some tea," and the woman led him to a small office attached to the back of the hangar.

"My husband went to seminary with one of the missionaries in Cerro Verde. It was their first post. Getting turned out, they felt like they'd failed." Calm as she was white, she seemed to gaze right through Paul.

"For whatever it's worth, I promise you they didn't fail because of Orlando Zavalla."

"Do you know the doctor well?"

"We went to medical school together."

"I spent some time in Cerro Verde," the woman said. "Doctor Zavalla certainly is a—fascinating man." The woman paused, and seemed torn between dueling immensities. "I think his intelligence could work against him in Cerro Verde, though. The place is so very remote." She looked through Paul again. "I fear the doctor's convictions might be, well, unsettled."

Paul sipped the tea. "He's a searcher, if that's what you mean."

"Yes. Very much so," the woman said. "But it can be very disruptive, the isolation. It can also be a gift." She considered for a moment. "I'm afraid the last missionaries were not prepared for it."

She was dreadfully pale for living in the tropics. Thin blue veins stood out on her thin white arms.

"Do you know the parable of the prodigal son?" she asked.

The conversation and the woman were condensing his uneasiness. "I need to know if Orlando is still in Cerro Verde."

"Yes, he is—so far as we know."

Paul looked confused.

"There hasn't been much news out of Cerro Verde for months now, but we'd surely have heard if the doctor had gone."

"How do I get there?"

"So you're going, then?"

"Yes."

That news seemed to deliver her of some cached worry, and she spoke louder and faster now: "Tramp steamers go to and from the mine every couple of hours, and smaller boats go all the way to Raul, where the doctor used to work. It's another fifty miles to Cerro Verde, and I don't know how you'd get there. But you've got to pass through Raul in any event. I think the doctor has some friends there, and they should help you—if they can."

Paul got to his feet. "Thanks. You've been kind."

The woman smiled cautiously, the smile of a child, before the world intruded. "It's not a safe place you're going to. The Indians are violent by nature, and they've been horribly abused." Seeing this had no effect on Paul, her eyes bore through him for a last time and her voice seemed to come from some deep and secret part of her. "I pray nothing has happened to the doctor."

The woman's directions led Paul to a wharf on the southern shore of the Rio Madeira, so wide that looking across it was like looking out to sea, the steamy, torpid water melding into a rain-blown void five miles out. A fleet of tramp steamers traveled continuously between the wharf and the Macunaima mine, some miles up the Rio Madeira and another two hours up a tributary. A steamer was overdue, judging by the dozens of men jostling and pacing on the creaky launch. The men—not one woman among them—were open as the sky, locked into the same crapshoot, every man knowing where the other was going and why. These garimpeiros were itinerant gold miners, burned dark by the sun, lean, cabled muscles from ferocious manual labor, covered in earth-stained, buttonless rags. The air was thick with the heady reek of bodies and auspicious talk full of foreign words Paul could not grasp, save the much-repeated "oro." Even the few rich men among them felt tense without their tattered clothes and outside their fellow ranks, so they traveled with the rest, where their prestige meant something—fortune's few sporting gold medallions big as a fist or Rolex President watches, and always, the raft of boot-lickers surrounding them.

Standing alone, duffel between his legs, Paul sighted right up the gut of the mighty river, far into the highlands. Lightning cracked so far in the distance he couldn't even hear it, could only see forked yellow veins strobing the ancient forest where a Venezuelan doctor, a free-lancer, worked the Methodists' claim. That Orlando still remained was rub enough; that he'd continued on his own behalf boiled the pilot's blood. The pilot—a cross on one shoulder and a boulder on the other. But the woman was different. Orlando's voice had touched her life, as she seemed sad to remember. But she seemed to know something else that made Paul feel every passing minute more acutely. He breathed easier seeing the boat pulling up to the launch.

The tramp steamer was not a steamer at all, rather a passenger barge, a greasy rust bucket belching soot from its clanking diesel, its open, ninety-square-foot deck a quilt of pot-iron patches darned over a hull so gouged and corroded that if so much as a single spot-weld ever let go, the entire ten tons of shuddering rubbish would crash like a house of iron cards. It had no guardrail or retaining wall, so the second it came within jumping range the launch became a wild frieze of men swarming aboard, garimpeiros all—but Paul—and the rush continued until bare heels ringed the iron deck and actually hung nervously overboard in some places and you couldn't have driven a nail between the half-naked, jostling, jabbering, grubby and sweat-soaked knot of humanity. The barge sounded its horn and swung out into the slow current, chugging for the promised land. With no place to sit or even turn, sixty-five people just stood, an inch away from sodomy. Then the sky cut loose and everyone sighed because the squall killed the blistering heat welling off the iron deck.

Impounded somewhere near the middle, Paul watched a walleyed teenager hold open court with every man around him. When he threw his head back and laughed, Paul saw thirty-two gold teeth. However much he had made, Paul knew it would never be enough because all these men wanted the same thing. They wanted more. At six-foot-three, Paul could peer over the heads of most aboard, and after two hours he watched amazed as the barge swerved extravagantly around an increasing colony of noisy craft, large and small, anchored in the river. Finally the barge pulled alongside one of the boats—twofold larger than most—and close to thirty men chucked their burlap bags to friends across the water, then stepped, jumped, even swam over to the facing deck overflowing with smoking, gyrating pumps and motors and a hive of clambering workers mud-encrusted and stripped to the waist. Teenaged divers wearing only underwear and dragging crude vacuum hoses plunged into the water to fight currents and dive deep to the river bottom to dredge gravel and silt. Twelve men shoulder-to-shoulder picked and panned through a chain of sluice boxes running the length of the hull as other men with screens and hoop-cloths and tiny fine-meshed sieves strained the viscous brown dross spewing off the stern of the boat and back into the river. On an upper deck a man wearing a gas mask bent over a huge wok set above a small coal fire, shuffling the contents of a blackened kettle like a Chinese cook, his eyes streaming from the mercury fumes. On both bow and stern two sloe-eyed men kept keen vigil with Thompson-type auto shotguns held across their bare chests.

The passenger barge pulled away and chugged on, wending its way through a logjam of other boats moored in the current, each one a frantic snarl of pumps and hoses and divers and panners.

Its number cut in half, the crowd loosened on deck and fell into cliques leaving Paul quite alone in a strange world. He moved back against the bridge and a tarpaulin-covered box, shaking some blood back into his feet and legs, numb from the idle standing. He felt along his kidneys and spleen, his liver, something he'd been doing periodically, almost unconsciously, for several weeks. That he never felt anything, even the slightest pang, made his condition seem more wolfish—this sneaky, inexorable cad of a disease, afraid to show its face. As he sat back on the box, several garimpeiros shot him queer looks.

It seemed like yesterday that he'd finished medical school in Venezuela and returned to Montana to do his residency. And it seemed like yesterday that he'd let his pride lure him into a fist-fight with Trevor Novak. The reasons didn't matter. Trevor was dead, and Paul had done it. He'd been in flight ever since, for the most part slaving in emerald mines deep in the Venezuelan rain forest. When a tumor forced him to the hospital in Maracaibo, and he found out he had leukemia, he knew that his options had finally run out—until Orlando's mother came and took him back to the Rancho Zavalla to recover. The tumor was a small one and he bounced back quickly, figuring to have several good months left before a creeping, implacable sloth overtook him. He could go to Caracas or Ciudad Bolívar and get blasted with chemotherapy, watch his balls wither and his hair fall out and be dead in six months anyway. Instead, he was staking everything on Orlando Zavalla de Fonseca, whom he'd gone to medical school with in Caracas. His effect on Paul was profound because he'd always favored Paul's audience; but anyone who had heard Orlando's facile handling of quantum mechanics, the death of God, or just his thoughts about a horse cantering across a plowed field, knew they were hearing an inspired man, interested in universal questions over private ones. Only if Paul could find him, he thought, could he sort through enough to stop running and dare to live. But some part of him wanted desperately to charge ahead and to keep charging, straight into a furious Indian or an insuperable rapid, because then he could fight something. And only in this way might he go out through a final burst of will, or rage, which to Paul Hudson, amounted to the same thing.

"Yo. Mira. You there," came a voice. "Deutsch? Francais? American?" the voice went on. "You must be one or the other."

Paul turned and looked toward the voice coming from the bridge, just a small platform elevated above the deck. Next to the steersman stood a grousy little man with wire-rimmed glasses, an oversized New York Knicks T-shirt and an East Coast twang in his voice.

"You speak English?"

Paul nodded.

"Well, come on up." Paul glanced around him. The garimpeiros were pointing to various boats and laughing and cursing them and each other. Paul grabbed his duffel, circled around and climbed six steps up to the bridge.

The man with the voice met Paul with his hand extended. "Joao Kessel, New York," he said, wringing Paul's hand like a pump handle. "Upstate, if you're wondering."

Paul wasn't. He wondered how another American ended up on that barge, and why they both were standing next to the helmsman—a nervous mulatto with the nub of a soggy black cheroot clenched between his rotting teeth.

"Where you headed—"

"Paul."

"Where you going, Paul?"

"To Raul."

Joao looked at him guardedly, and lit a cigarette. "Raul?"

"You ever been there?"

Joao huffed hard on the cigarette. "Not hardly." The comment dangled in the heat.

Paul finally said, "I have a friend there, a doctor in the clinic."

"You must be a doctor as well, then?" Joao almost begged the question.

Paul paused, and answered, "Yes."

Joao inexplicably chuckled in relief, hit his cigarette again, flicked the butt into the river and mumbled, "I smoke too much." Then he reached down and fetched three sodas from a cooler at their feet, handing the steersman and Paul each one. The barge rattled on through the haze.

Joao explained himself as a writer, there to research a book. Born in Rio, his family immigrated when he was six, and he'd grown up in Mamaroneck, New York. Freed up by the sales of his last seven books—wily spy thrillers found in better airports from New Delhi to Winnipeg—he'd returned to his homeland for story ideas. But after a week kicking around the area he decided to go with his first nonfiction book, "because even Milton couldn't embellish this place." His scathing cynicism colored everything he saw, and there seemed little he didn't see, quickly and truly. He remembered little of Brazil and had hardly been on the Madeira, so things were as new to him as they were to Paul—or had been seven weeks before, when he'd first arrived. "I'm more amazed than a month ago," Joao said, gesturing across the water. "Around us is the biggest gold rush and the vilest fiasco in the history of man."

Paul nodded, noting the thousands of boats choking the river.

"This rio has rapids and it has prospectors and it's a toss-up which is trickier," Joao said. There were daily killings over fixing scales, claim jumping, filching the boss's dust under the finger-nails. Scores were settled underwater—air hoses slashed, anchor lines cut. Many divers died from embolisms, bursting up from the muddy water with crossed eyes and great ruby bubbles on their foreheads. Others got a pound of gold a day. "But it's all small change compared to the Macunaima mine," Joao added.

The mine, only nine months old, was considered richer than even the Serra Palada site, near Maraba, a tropical Klondike from which the garimpeiros had already clawed out over a billion dol-lars in gold. The river dredging started after all the Macunaima plots were claimed, seven months back.

"You won't believe what it looks like," Joao said. "Nobody can."

"I'll take your word for it."

"You'll see it. There's only one boat that goes upriver from the mine, and it leaves in the morning— if it leaves at all."

"You sure about that?"

"Quite."

Paul didn't want to waste a minute of his life inspecting a gold mine, especially after six hours on the barge, but he finally warmed up to the man who handed him another soda and lipped another cigarette. Tense as a weasel, Joao seemed gracious enough—though awfully sore about something—and his running acid gloss helped pass the miles.

Joao fumbled through his pockets for matches. "If you think all those garimpeiros are down there because they have to be, think again. A couple of them could buy this tub and everyone on it." He pointed out the wall-eyed kid with the fifty-carat smile. "Aluizio Crespo. Used to shovel shit at a pig ranch in Paranangua. Last Christmas he hit a vein and pulled out three million worth of gold in seven days. Bought a waterfront hotel on the Copacabana and signed the check with a thumbprint."

The boat continued its labored slalom through the clangoring gold barges. A driving rain soaked everyone and after several lightning blasts, it stopped just as suddenly as it had begun. The snarling clouds parted and sunlight blazed down so strong Paul could feel it sear his arms and neck. Since the wharf, the left shoreline had stretched as a continuous weeping ulcer, the vulgar, splintered stumps running from the water up to high places and distant fires, all undergrowth torched off and the primal orange mud a quagmire so revolting that when the winds shifted, knees buckled and eyes watered. With each sorry mile Paul felt a little of himself whittled off and burnt to cinders as well. He looked up the river toward a future hazy as the highlands that, ten miles off, seemed to devour this great fouled watercourse in a welter of smoke and fire.

Joao squinted at the ravaged shoreline. "It gets worse before it gets any better."

Joao spotted the military launch just after they'd veered off the Madeira and onto the Rio Arce; he and Paul watched it till it pulled alongside the barge. A lieutenant, dark and angular in his camo fatigues and knock-off aviator shades, stood square and heroic in the bow, as if someone played a drumroll in his honor. He clambered up onto the barge like he'd done it before, muddy boots bicycling.

"Just look at that dip-shit," Joao mumbled. "Spent his entire thirty years trying to grow a mustache and only has that silly bit of fuzz to show for it."

Paul watched the crowd below slowly part for the lieutenant and asked, "What's up?"

"Whiff patrol. Happens every trip."

"Whiff?"

"Relax. It doesn't concern us," Joao said.

The lieutenant mingled around, painting the deck with a vast fake grin and searching for the slightest nervousness from the men, who ignored him as a fool and were annoyed at the delay. He poked through a couple of bags, and eventually climbed up to the bridge.

Portuguese and Spanish are very much the same—save the accent—and Paul, reared by Chilean immigrants in Montana, knew Spanish as well as English; but the phrases exchanged between Joao and the lieutenant were so guttural Paul only made out "writer," "book" and "mine." Then Joao explained Paul as a doctor visiting friends in a clinic upstream—or so it sounded. The lieutenant studied Paul's passport for a long minute, returned it to him, assayed the steersman with his sham grin and backpedaled to the deck.

He took a couple of slow steps back toward his launch, then stopped and studied the tarp-covered box. He asked a question and one of the garimpeiros drew his finger across his throat: A dead man lay under that tarp. He asked something else and the garimpeiros shook their heads. Nobody knew the deceased or where he came from. The lieutenant went over and shook the tarp off the timber coffin, kicked it, heard the departed slide around, grinned, and again asked about the dead man and again the men said they didn't know. His grin tightened at the edges; then he yelled for a machete and started prying at the nailed lid.

Paul noticed the steersman rained sweat and had chewed his cheroot to the quick. Twice the lieutenant snapped the tip off the machete trying to force the lid. Finally he opened it enough to order four garimpeiros to pull it all the way off.

Inside lay a fiftyish, barrel-chested man in a tight black suit, newly deceased, his milk-chocolate eyes open and forever, his arms crossed over his chest. Feeling along the black suit, the lieutenant tried to draw back a rigored limb and the grey corpus shifted in the box. Two privates came aboard and hefted the body from the coffin and it returned unto this world stiff as a plaster statue drawn from a wax mold. The privates laid it on the deck, put a boot each on the torso and the lieutenant heaved on the left arm till the shoulder snapped and the rigid limb flopped back like a rag doll. The lieutenant repeated his work on the other arm, then yanked at the black suit coat: sewn shut. A pass with a jackknife and the snug coat popped open exposing a grisly slash, crudely sutured with thin cordage, running from clavicle down across the belly and into the black trousers.

"Christo. Doctor must have borrowed a chainsaw for that autopsy," Joao muttered.

Paul peered over the bridge for a better look and said, "That's not from any autopsy."

The lieutenant felt about the corpse's bloated, lumpy torso, then he suddenly slashed at the taut stitches. The chest burst open like a clamshell and several plastic-wrapped parcels popped from the scarlet cavity. The lieutenant's grin stretched to his ears.

"Oh, shit," Joao said.

The lieutenant drew his pistol, fired a shot into the air and thirty-five men instantly kissed the iron deck. Several other soldiers swarmed on board from their launch. One corporal moved to the corpse and began extracting more kilos, reaching as deep as the kneecaps in the gutted frame. A tall pile of plastic-wrapped parcels soon lay on deck and the corpse was just a hollow skin valise with head and floppy arms. The kilos were stacked into the coffin and loaded onto the military boat, the corpse flung into the river. The lieutenant climbed up to the bridge, waved Joao and Paul away with his pistol and, smiling again, handcuffed the steersman to the helm.

Escorted by the military launch, the barge chugged on toward the mine.

"That steersman's a goner," Joao said to Paul, the two men huddled by the stern.

"And us?"

"They could care less about us. They got what they wanted. Must have been tipped off."

According to Joao, much of the gold rush was fueled by cocaine. White powder for gold powder. Jacked by the drug, garimpeiros could work longer hours, eat less, make more. "Narcotrafficantes" controlled the trade until the military recently moved into the mine. Now it was open war between the two, the generals looking to cash in either by taking a cut or stealing the goods outright and having junior officers peddle them. Freelancers caught trying to deal the generals out were robbed, emasculated and tossed in the river. Dozens had suffered this fate,

"But no matter," Joao said. "The shit will keep flowing over the Bolivian divide and down the river so long as there's a cruzeiro to buy it and a nose to whiff it."

Late that afternoon, the barge gained the mine. Just as Joao had predicted, the steersman was dragged off and the other passengers simply streamed ashore without a question asked. Joao offered to put Paul up for the night and to see him onto the boat heading upriver the next morning. Paul had no choice. Joao took Paul's elbow and they trudged through the mud to get a look at the subject of Joao's new book: the Macunaima mine.

The forest was razed for five square miles, the fringe a splintered dam of logs crackling with orange flames and hissing in the downpour, smoke billowing off and into the low grey pall. The stench of sewage clashed with the crisp smell of worked earth and a frenzied multitude—ex-cons, ex-barbers, ex-doctors, even ex-priests, tens of thousands strong and swimming in swirling mud—stormed around with savage hope on their faces. The smoke and racket swelled as Paul and Joao trudged closer to the massive open pit and peered inside.

Two hundred feet below loomed a vision from a fevered dream—40,000 men, nearly naked, glazed in swelter and blood and deluge, a thunderous seething mud hole of flashing shovels and writhing backs attacking a flush grid of claims averaging ten foot square. Thirty men, fused hip to hip and ass to ass, worked each plot. Most resembled complex bunkers, tiered and ever collapsing and no sooner dug back out. Paul saw men slither into foxholes and others dragged out by the ankles, bags of pay dirt in their hands, and he saw men rabidly digging and shoveling and swinging axes and mauls and levering huge stones with pry bars, and he saw one man hammer a shelf of living rock with a hatchet, and he saw a man get a pickax through the foot and another man turn to piss but there was no place to turn, so he pissed onto the very mud another man trawled and the men fought and the one opened the other's forehead up to the bone and a dozen other men joined the fight but the surrounding throng hardly looked and never stopped. A stream of 5,000 men wended through the throng in an endless loop, humping ninety-pound bags of dirt from the sump up a forty-degree slope, legs shin-deep and staggering up the mud, finally stumbling to the summit of the mountain of tailings and dropping their bags and collapsing and lying as if dead but for their heaving ribs. He saw the dirt dumped or sluiced or panned by 10,000 other men, while the carriers rose slowly from the mud and joined the loop for another load, back into the wallowing brown madness, every single task done by hand, the toil and wretchedness heightened by the taskmasters' rough handling of the workers who had a slim-to-none chance of getting rich—40,000 muddy slaves, rabid with gold fever, buoyed by the dozen millionaires gamboling around them. He'd seen violence and greed and lust, had seen men kill and be killed over all three, but Paul had never seen anything like this. The bottom of that pit was a moral wilderness so profound that no conscience, no soul, no God could endure it. Only the garimpeiros could. Somewhere down there was their icon and their redemption. Somewhere down there was gold.

"I saw a boy die here last week," Joao said. "Tunnel collapsed. He was still breathing when they dragged him out, but he died before they got his name. They buried him in the jungle, I think." Joao continued looking below, as he'd done for the last seven weeks.

At the perimeter, above and beyond the blazing shoal of trees, Paul noticed a lone spoonbill perched in a solitary jacaranda tree, motionless, peering down at the filthiest scramble for loot to ever profane the face of man and earth. Looking back into that hole, Paul thought that he saw his own life. But if he were to strike pay dirt, it'd be well upstream, at the last place on no map.

"Let's go," Paul said.

They trudged through the Plaza of Lies, where the miners gathered at night to recount their doubtful tales, past a shanty brothel, young mulattas from Rio and São Paulo peering cannily from dark nooks inside—"Gram of gold for half an hour," said Joao. Paul noticed that many miners carried pistols.

"They use them to celebrate every nugget found, or to settle debts," Joao said. Owners never paid their laborers cash money, rather points in their respective claims, redeemable at a future strike. Pilots, merchants, doctors, even the prostitutes were "paid" in this manner. Following a recent strike worth over four million, close to thirty people stepped forward with vouchers totaling over two-hundred and thirty percent of the take, and things got so crazy that the owner had to settle up his lesser accounts with his gun. "Just last month there was so much shooting at night you couldn't sleep," Joao said. But now the military had arrived and much of the unofficial shooting had stopped.

They reached the sprawling shantytown soaking wet. Laborers were already streaming in from the pit and collapsing under plastic tarps, foremen stumbling into crude shacks. Behind the shacks rose a row of box dwellings belonging to the donos, or claim owners. Joao trudged on to the biggest structure, set above the swimming mud on a cluster of carnauba stumps, its reed walls teeming with black ants, a brown curtain of water cascading off its tin roof. Joao teetered up a notched log, pushed through a drape of beads hanging in the doorway and went inside. Paul followed.

Four men, straight out of the pit, sat around a small plastic table playing dominos and drinking from a bottle of white, unmarked spirits. Though filthy and coarse as the lowliest shoveler, the gaudy gold medallions and watches and rings and the fat stack of 10,000 cruzeiro notes on the table said it all. Two Coleman lanterns hissed overhead. Otherwise, the home of Guilhermino Arantes was empty.

The twenty-three-year-old son of subsistence farmers from Cuiabá, Guilhermino had dug out a nugget big as an attaché case. With it, he bought a rancho in Borba with 12,000 head of cattle. Even gave his folks a job. As peons. The central figure in Joao's book, he'd rented the writer a back room. Guilhermino and the other three men, none over thirty, glanced up from their dominos, stunned to see a blond-haired, green-eyed gringo there.

Joao introduced Paul as a doctor and a close friend from the States. But when asked his destination, Raul was cautiously mentioned and the smiles fell straight off the men's faces.

Paul looked over at Joao and said, "I'm going to Cerro Verde, actually."

The garimpeiros understood nothing except "Cerro Verde," but the name had barely left Paul's mouth when Guilhermino sprang up and began windmilling his arms and glaring at Paul and hollering at Joao: "Suma con ele daqui!"—get the gringo the hell out of here.

Joao's hands came up in defense, but all four men were shouting at him and cutting the air with their hands and murdering Paul with their black eyes. Yet Joao stood firm, yelling right back: "Doctor—friend—another doctor—good man—clinic," these the few words Paul could make out. He was impressive in his own way, this fiery little New Yorker going word for word with big muddy throwaways who would slash a man's throat for a gilt toothpick. The four garimpeiros slowly sat back down, appeased for the moment, but anxious. Still glaring at Paul, Guilhermino barked to Joao to hide the gringo and clear him out at first light. Paul wasn't certain those were the miners exact words, but his drift was clear enough. Guilhermino shooed the Americans off with a flick of his hand and returned to his dominos. Joao took Paul's arm and quickly retreated to a corner room stacked with magazines, books, papers, a typewriter and a cot.

Joao stoked the lantern and said, "For both our sakes, don't tell anybody else you're going to Raul, and certainly not to Cerro Verde."

Paul looked perfectly confused.

"Cocaine," Joao said, his hands outstretched. "It passes right through there, straight from Bolivia. A strange gringo going to the border sounds too much like a man out to peddle blow behind the generals' backs; and even if he's not, he'd have to be crazy to go up there."

"I'm going to a clinic, Joao."

"Fine," Joao said, stripping off his wet clothes. "But nobody knows that for sure but you."

"I better find somewhere else to sleep," Paul said. "I can only compromise your position by staying here."

Joao didn't answer, simply fretted around the little berth, shuffling aside books and heaps of manuscript, and finally said, "Nobody cares what you're doing here unless you mention Cerro Verde." He gave Paul a sideways glance. "You are a doctor."

"Barely," Paul said.

Joao wrung out his shirt in the corner. Then he sat down on the cot, started massaging his knee and said, "I blew out two cartilages playing hoops last winter." He kept rubbing his knee. "Now I'm hobbling around with just the one left."

"You've got none left," Paul said, answering the bait, "Only two cartilages in the knee, Joao."

"And a surgeon dug both of them out this October." Joao chuckled in relief.

"Orthoscope, by the looks of those four scars."

"You got it," Joao said. "Friend, excuse me for doubting you, but the layers of bullshit around this place start at the bottom of that pit and climb to the clouds. I try and keep it out of this little room, though, even if I've got to sleep outside." Joao reached under his cot and brought out a bottle of Bordeaux. "I've been saving this."

Joao rustled up some fried rice, guavas and alligator pears, and once he got into the wine, his restless enthusiasm returned. He turned to his reference books, anthropology texts, grid maps, magazines.

According to his sources—spread out over the floor and the cot—Cerro Verde was recognized not so much as a place, but as the whole area at the headwaters of the Rio Arce and straddling the Brazilian/Bolivian border. Joao scanned a little further, whistled, and said, "Take some pretty bold missionaries to stay up there. And lucky."

"They're gone," Paul said.

"Gone where?"

"Back to Minnesota. Driven off over a year ago."

"And your friend?"

"Still there."

"Alone?"

"Not alone. There's Indians."

"Oh, there's Indians," Joao said, glossing over one of three books on his lap: "Plenty of Indians. Kaxarari, Pakahanova, and Urupa tribes." He whistled again.

"Whatever," Paul said impatiently.

"Are you this crazy or that stupid?"

"You been up there or something?"

Joao studied Paul for a moment, bemused at his recklessness. Most likely, he just didn't know.

"Don't take my word for it," Joao said. He thumbed over some text, and stopped: "'...and industrial exploitation of their native lands has driven a dozen different groups, all traditional enemies, into the Cerro Verde territories, resulting in murder and mayhem, famine, dreadful epidemics and appalling psychological shock.' A man alone up there is crowbait, my friend."

"We got letters from him," Paul said, "after the missionaries were gone."

"And?"

"And he was doing just fine."

Just fine were hardly the words to describe Orlando's peculiar letters; but accepting it as the most incredible fact, Joao's imagination ran away with the whole thing. He couldn't hear enough about the man who took the slow boat to Europe and returned on the Concorde with a fistful of degrees, the quadrilingual who'd probed grey matter with a laser, the atomic age genius who'd blown off bids from governors to "go bush" for unknown reasons; and Joao made the wildest guesses about Orlando's long silence.

"He's just a man doing a job," Paul finally said.

Perhaps; but it was the why of it all that captivated Joao, who put the book down, lit another cigarette, blew out a stream and said, "You've got to be a little crazy, a little desperate to ever come to a place like this. And you've got to suffer a little, die a little, go insane a little to survive it. And you know I hate it here. I detest it. But I hate it less than what I left behind."

Joao checked the wine bottle. Still empty.

"A couple months here, Paul, and you can never return to the way it was, and that's the whole point of it. I'm staying until I'm sure that when I go back I won't recognize the place, and nobody will recognize me. I suspect your doctor friend came here for similar reasons. But I'm just playing at it. He's living it."

All this second-guessing only made Paul's lingering questions more severe. "What time does that boat leave tomorrow?"

"Early," Joao said. "We better get our stuff together."

"We?"

♦ ♦ ♦

Through a stretch of forest cut absolutely flat, Paul sighted a distant peak to the east, unrolled the map, and penciled another eighth inch over the black line of the Rio Arce. Because of the current, the last few marks were only slight dashes. A lot of twisting river still lay between him and Orlando. Paul handed the map back to Joao, and stood back up in the bow, his eyes fixed upriver. The rain beat down so hard and so hot it stung their skin.

"What if your friend is dead?" Joao asked, tucking the map back into his pack. "Then what?"

"I'll find out when I get there," Paul said, not looking over. Joao had talked around that question for three days, and Paul's answer confirmed what he already suspected: Paul Hudson was going to Cerro Verde come monsoon or a thousand arrows. If the barge they were on broke down, he'd swim there; and if the racket of the pitiful craft was any indication, he might have to. The grubby little boat seemed to move along by divine will, for a lesser force could never drive it. Half the size of the last barge, it clanked and clanged like its flywheel was falling off—which it was. The pilot was an antique negro, all leathern skin and bones. His gaze, always straight ahead, had that set changelessness that comes from years of silence and solitude. In three days, he hadn't said five words, though when the engine sounded like it couldn't survive another stroke, he'd grunt something to his young Caboclo assistant who'd instantly disappear below deck. Horrendous hammering would sound out. An hour later the kid would crawl back on deck, smeared in grease and reeking of benzene and bilge water. Otherwise, the kid worked a hand-crank bailer every waking minute. Perhaps fourteen, he had a long lick of shiny black hair and strips of tire thonged to the floors of his feet. Paul hadn't seen him eat a thing in three days.

The deck overflowed with fifty-five-gallon fuel drums, cases of Pepsi-Cola and canned foods, outboard motors, rolls of sheet metal—even a plastic Christmas tree—things ordered by the thinning outposts, rubber plantations and settlements along the way.

The human cargo had thinned to Paul, Joao, the pilot and his exhausted assistant. Several days before it included half a dozen Caboclo and Indian kids, amongst the weariest Paul had ever seen. Prodded downstream by brutal poverty, or even indentured as the result of a father's dice game with a garimpeiro, the kids were thrown straight into the pit, surrounded by strange miners and a strange language, fed strange food, made to work like animals; they sickened, collapsed, were beaten, and eventually crawled back upstream far worse than they had come and never one cruzeiro richer. They'd get off the boat at the vaguest shoals, find the footpath and stumble into the fastness, never looking back.

Two days above the Macunaima mine they passed the last boat scouring the riverbed for gold. Another day and they were beyond the last panner and the final logging camp and into primary terrain. The forest reared higher, the river narrowed, the current quickened, the boat slowed and Paul grew more restless.

Hugging the bank against the current, the boat ground around a spit freckled with polished stones and plied through curtains of green light slanting down from the closing trees. The Caboclos called it "la salon verde," the green room. Gnarled ropes looped down from the heights, flecked with black orchids and strangler figs. Several giant, uprooted trees floated by, and now and again the negro would veer around islets of rushes in river shallows. Croaking bullfrogs sounded from reeking streams emptying into the river, and twice the boat chugged past coves of mangrove through whose riotous roots blared the mad chorus of howler monkeys.

Joao spent hours studying the small settlements they passed, the sparse, meager homes of the Caboclos, the river people of the lower Arce whose thatched hovels, set high on piles, overlooked the river from above the monsoon line. Then he'd scribble furiously in his journal, fold it shut in mid-sentence and just stare into the forest gliding by.

"There is something nameless and essential in this great green room, where water and wood reach back 100 million years. But they'll dig and hose and sift and burn till it's all an arid ruin of bones and ashes, a few fat Generals sitting on clear-cut stumps, like dense Hamlets, silly gold nugget in hand, wondering how it all happened. Then where will people like me go, people who need to get to the far places of the earth?"

Paul read this last sentence again and slowly handed the journal back to Joao.

"I just started keeping a diary last month," Joao said. "Ever kept one, Paul?"

"Never have."

"Figured you hadn't. I can tell you, I've learned more about myself in these last few weeks—thumbing through what I've been scribbling in here—than I've learned in the last twenty years. You might consider a diary sometime, if that kind of thing interests you."

Just then horrendous clanging sounded from below deck. The negro shut down to quarter power, but the racket got louder still. The boy hurried below and a salvo of hammer blows rang out, but the engine still sounded like it was flying apart with each piston stroke. Fighting the current, the pilot finally pulled over at a small, abandoned settlement half a mile upstream, and tied off to a cannonball tree arching over the river. In the clearing, several tattered, oblong huts perched on palm pylons.

Paul paced about the bow while the negro and the kid worked below. Then, both he and Joao were forced off the boat, as within half an hour every inch of open deck was covered with the entire top end of a savaged V-6 engine. The old negro mumbled a couple sentences to Joao and made a motion toward the huts, handed him a sledgehammer, then went back below to the hammering.

"He says the sun's going down and they need a fire to work by," Joao said. "He's got to make Raul by Thursday and can't waste a day on repairs. We can get the wood off those shacks."

"And the people?"

Joao glanced toward the huts and said, "They all died last year. Measles."

The sepulchral hush inside those empty huts seemed to carry the sighs of forgotten lives, amplified by a wooden basin intricately braided into the reed walls, a carved stool, a manioc grater leaning in the corner, as if carelessly left there yesterday. Paul felt ashamed to be dismantling all this for a fire, and for a time just listened to the shadows. Meanwhile, Joao laid into the walls with the sledgehammer. In an hour, they had a good stack of bamboo, reeds and hardwood joisting, and a shoreline fire licking thirty feet into the air. Behind them, all that remained of the huts were a dozen pylons rearing from red soil.

Stripped to shorts and running sweat, the two Americans worked the fire to keep the light high enough to slant into the boat. The sky was starless and jet black.

"Why do you have to get to the far places of the world, Joao?" Paul asked, stirring the fire with a bamboo staff.

"Everybody has a place he needs to get to."

"Well, what did you hope to find?"

Joao glanced into the dark forest, at the fire, at the silhouette of the negro yelling down to the kid whose hammer blows grew louder and faster.

"This, I guess."

Paul fixed Joao for a beat, coughed out a little astounded laugh and asked, "This?" Then he tossed another armload of bamboo onto the fire and sat silently back on the clay bank.

Joao flicked his cigarette into the fire and said, "People like me can reach a point when it looks like we've got it all, but in fact the world is lost. There's no good, no bad, no hope. We don't live, we only carry on, baffled, like a wounded animal. So we come out here, where the animal can recover, because there's a great cure in nature—if only we can find it. We might hate it here, we might suffer, but when we can finally go back, we're cured."

That "cured" ricocheted around Paul's head like a bullet in a barrel. He got up and pitched more bamboo onto the fire, and his mind drifted back to the Ranchero Zavalla—so recently the finest spread in Estado Anzoátuegui. But now, as Paul had been astonished to see, the fences were peeling and cracked; the cane grass, once trimmed daily by forty hands, and now gone two years, had rioted over the grounds; creeping weeds overran the tiled foyer; the fountains were full of black rainwater and haloed with mosquitos; the Arabian horses were gone, the stables empty.

Paul knew Orlando's mother, Doña Dometilda, had fetched him from the hospital in Maracaibo and brought him to the ranchero for reasons beyond merely recovering from what he told her was a minor surgery, reasons Paul would let her tell him in her own time. Neither Orlando, nor the wreckage of the ranch, were mentioned during the flight from Maracaibo to Barcelona, or the thirty-minute cab ride to San Tomé. Only apologies that she had had to let the car go the previous year because she could no longer afford the chauffeur. To see this superb, proud woman, the very article of nobility and benevolence, courageously admit her bankruptcy, was dispiriting. And to see the mansion, a safe harbor whose fond associations kept alive in Paul the notion that human life could actually amount to something—to see it utterly gone to seed—struck Paul so deeply that his own worries seemed smaller by contrast.

The mansion, once bustling with society's illustrious, was now gloomy and drab. All had decayed but the study, which had retained its continental furnishings, frescoes and statuettes, and its grandeur. This high-ceilinged rosewood and marble chamber, a shrine to the few great men and women who had passed through the ages, remained the last pillar of the crumbling Zavalla legacy, and Doña Dometilda had preserved it perfectly.

The walls were lined with over 5,000 classic works of literary immortals, and their presence in the room seemed as tangible as Paul's memories of the many nights he had passed there with Orlando, who with waving arms would fashion a world unto itself, a luminous orb spinning breathlessly on the finger of its creator. In that room, Paul found an atmosphere of contingency, where he could encompass and reconcile the extremes in his life, and could reinvent himself, under Orlando's tutelage, the way he wanted to be. But the thing that most enchanted him, and which often sparked Orlando's most inspired moments, lay overhead, high in the vaulted apse, where many lustrous bits of rock and mineral had been arranged in such a manner as to make an image that suggested a man gazing down at them—not a specific man, or even a possible man, yet more like a man than anything else. What the mosaic projected was an artist's idea of a universal seer, and in contemplating all the subtleties of his gaze, said Orlando, one could become enlightened. Without contemplating this feeling, and others like it, a man would perish. The few who had grasped the subtleties lived on in the 5,000 volumes lin-ing the walls.

Paul and Doña Dometilda took their meals in the library, served to them by the last remaining maid, who had been with the Zavallas for nearly thirty years and had nowhere else to go. On the second night, when Paul had recovered as well as he ever would, and had brought all his eagerness into the room with him, Doña tried to explain.

Orlando's father, Don José, had invested heavily in natural gas futures just after Venezuela helped establish OPEC. The gov-ernment immediately borrowed billions from the World Bank for "domestic projects," the money soon in the pockets of certain generals and governors, of course. When gas prices plummeted worldwide, the country defaulted on its loans, the bolivar shot through the roof, and Don José, God bless his eternal soul, was ruined. The shock and dishonor killed him.

Francisco, the eldest Zavalla, took charge of the estate, and quickly parceled off hunks of the ranch—not to restore the family, but to maintain his fast life in Puerto La Cruz. Outraged, Orlando took legal action. The Magistrate (one of the biggest buyers of Zavalla land) ruled in Francisco's favor, and things grew worse between the two brothers. Ultimately, Orlando fought all comers, and lost on every count.

On a whim, or maybe just to get away, that Christmas vaca-tion Orlando joined the Friends of Brazil on a two-week humani-tarian venture to a remote clinic in Raul, on the Arce River, a trib-utary of the southern fork of the Amazon. According to Doña Dometilda, he returned a changed man—nothing dramatic, rather subtle little ripples only a mother would perceive—a little more pensive, and strangely intrigued about nothing he could put into words.

"And he went back?" Paul asked.

"Yes," Doña Dometilda said. In the next four months he twice applied for a leave of absence from the hospital and both times was refused. The big men were grooming him as a future Health Minister. Several political big men vied for his allegiance, and there was even talk about luring him from medicine altogether and maneuvering him toward a governorship or more. And Orlando had gone to the Amazon.

"So, he's still there?" Paul asked.

"Yes. I think he is," Doña Dometilda said, her voice trembling.

"You think?"

"Yes, of course he is. It's just, well, I haven't heard from Orlando in some time."

"How long, Señora?"

"There are no phones where Orlando is. And his letters must be flown out on a missionary plane, which does not go where he is so often."

"When was the last time you heard from Orlando, Señora?"

"It has been some time," she said, then covered her face with her hands.

"How long?"

She finally took her hands from her face. "Fourteen months." Her voice cracked, and she made no effort to hide the tears.

Doña Dometilda couldn't explain it. Paul could make no sense of it. Nobody could. Orlando had applied for leave and the hospital administrator, the Minister of Health—even the Vice-President of the Christian Democratic Front—all said relax, Señor Zavalla. You are the future. Some day you will serve on our boards, perhaps run the board, the Districto Federal, the whole goddam nation. It's entirely up to you how far you'll go. So Orlando Zavalla de Fonseca packed his bags and went farther than anyone could understand.

He knew what he was giving up. Leaving on his own terms was tantamount to spitting in the big men's faces. He'd had it all—or would have shortly—but if he ever came back now, they'd stick him in the boondocks and chuck him a loaf of sweet bread every month or so.

Paul wondered what the hell he'd seen on that first trip, why he'd jumped ship, why he'd seemed to have drowned. That bush planes rarely went to his remote clinic was one thing. But fourteen months? Paul could almost throw a rock to the neighboring

Brazilian border, and could walk to the Amazon in fourteen months. He started with Orlando's letters, dating back twenty-seven months, and neatly ordered inside an envelope marked: Mission Aviation Fellowship (MAF), Porto Velho, Brazil.

The first letters were long and personal, written to his mother, though parts seemed written to every man and woman on earth. The clinic was meager, but the people, called Caboclos, half Portuguese, half Indian, "are grateful for the little we can do for them."

Several months later, Orlando described a strenuous trip from his little clinic in Raul, "to the last place on no map," called Cerro Verde, up the last reaches of the Rio Arce at the Bolivian border, the final sanctuary for indigenous peoples "driven here by chainsaws, gold miners and soldiers." The mission consisted of two soon-to-retire missionaries and a French doctor who'd requested Orlando come upriver to help him fight an epidemic of intestinal worms.

Within a month, hypertension drove the Frenchman home, and the missionaries retired, replaced by "a repulsive pair of green gringos." Orlando reluctantly agreed to stay on until another doctor arrived from Ohio. Within a month, "these dispassionate impostors of God" were commanding him to "turn out the simple forest people and to minister to their converted few." It tortured him to sit by and watch "these blind bearers of light destroy what they profess to enlighten."

Then, following a gap of seven weeks, came another letter, Orlando describing his "new work" as a "most deserving challenge, my mind bursting with designs fitted to its magnitude." No mention of the missionaries. Six weeks passed, then came a letter so abstruse that trying to catch the meaning was like grabbing smoke.

"The Fact has prowled in my unconsciousness since my first trip to Raul," the letter ran. That was his "reason" for going back there, to drag this slippery Fact out of the wilderness, out of himself. The moment came after trekking ninety miles in seven days to inoculate a nomadic tribe of Caripunas. Returning to Cerro Verde, Orlando and his two Indian guides got caught in the cross fire of warring tribes, were forced into the barren highlands to escape. Four days stretched desperately into seven, five without water. Still two days from Cerro Verde, stumbling, lost, "more dead than alive, I became the thirst itself, and only the thirst. Then the thirst died, leaving the naked man facing the naked Fact. The Fact was only the wilderness, was only me; but it was also the last human truth. I understood, and in my understanding I became The Fact itself, and only The Fact." Paul reread this last bit several times. Then he translated it into English and still couldn't make sense of it.

Apparently, some days passed back in Cerro Verde before Orlando recovered enough to continue the letter with a weird passage about "the strength and clarity necessary to walk the jagged edge of The Fact," and of the "terror" of ever falling off. "That is my dream and my nightmare—falling off, and surviving."

Then a strange letter of a few disparate phrases—that he'd "dived into The Fact and fell out of its womb," had "found the courage to embrace its methods," and how The Fact was "beyond all judgement." The letter was signed, "Faithfully yours, Orlando." There was no correspondence beyond that.

After waiting two months for another letter, for any word whatsoever, Doña Dometilda tried directly contacting the MAF people in Porto Velho, who had forwarded Orlando's mail for all these months; but a dozen letters in as many weeks brought no response. Finally, she received a terse note from the MAF office saying they had "suspended operations" to Cerro Verde. A month later, a short letter arrived from the wife of one of the MAF pilots. The new missionaries had been driven out of Cerro Verde by hostile tribesmen. Her husband tried flying back in, but Indians had plugged the landing strip with palm stumps and he couldn't set down. The husband and several missionaries from the regional office in Brasilia tried to gain Cerro Verde by river, and both times were turned away by natives—attacked the second time. As far as the woman knew, Dr. Zavalla still worked in Cerro Verde—he was certainly there when the missionaries were stuffed into a dugout and sent downstream—but of course, it would be impossible to forward any more of his correspondence, et cetera, et cetera. "May God be with Doctor Zavalla," the note ended. That was ten months ago, and further letters from Doña Dometilda had gone unanswered. The MAF office in Porto Velho had no phone.

That night, Paul lay in bed and stared at the ceiling. For three mornings, he couldn't find a reason to get up. Each time he woke, he knew he was that much less, and less, until finally he'd wake up and be totally gone. He tried to fathom it, when he would become nothing, nowhere, dust, ashes, utter darkness; but his mind always took hold of wind, clouds, rain, light, because he could never grab hold of nothing. And through these thoughts the murky business about The Fact kept churning. Strange stuff, but that was just Orlando and his words. Nobody understood all of them anyway, not without him there to light them up. Paul used to live for those late nights in the dormitory, in the Zavalla study, walking along the beach in Maiquetía and Orlando lighting up the world. But now, the man everyone wanted a piece of was walking a jagged edge in the Amazon. Alone. What balls, Paul laughed to himself; but the laugh died in his throat when he remembered those letters were a year old. More than a year. And the last ones were God-awful weird. When he looked up, the ceiling had dropped another inch. He'd left for Cerro Verde the next afternoon.

All night the negro and the kid slaved over the engine, and all night Paul and Joao worked the fire, their huge shadows dancing over a somber screen of trees.

The wood gave out in the wee hours, and Paul and Joao took turns sledgehammering the palm pylons until they worked loose and they could draw them from the clayey soil and roll them down to the fire. Just past dawn, the engine fired over and the old negro waved them back aboard.

Behind them, the mountain of coals smoked and crackled. In a week, the rising monsoon would claim the cinders and the teeming jungle would continue advancing over the small clearing. Rain and wind would salt the ruin and in a matter of a few years, there would be nothing but a solitary pylon to tell a passing boat that people had lived there and that there they had died.

Rain beat down from one black cloud, the blood-red sun beside it. Steam welled off the moving water, dull, still-hanging, and so thick Paul could taste his own hot breath. Thunder clapped and volleyed down the green corridor, followed closely by sheets of blistering rain. The river would surge up two feet in ten minutes, and ten minutes later the sun was alone and filled half the sky. The negro forged on, his face pouring sweat but fixed.

They passed through a stratum of dark rock ledges extending far into the southern bank. The forest grew immense, and the slender isles between trees darker. Here and there the gloomy green wall was relieved by orange festoons dangling beneath the pao d'orco trees. Only occasionally did the grove break for small, black streams trickling into the river.

Late that afternoon the sky went ablaze between thin rags of clouds, the deep lime forest cutting across the vivid glare like a ruled line. The river mirrored the sky so precisely that the water shined like liquid gold, from which suddenly rose an Indian paddling downstream, a huge manatee in the floor of his dugout. His chin was smeared red with annatto and on both sides of his face a tattooed streak ran from the corner of his mouth to his temple. He seemed to neither ignore nor acknowledge them, simply paddled past, stroking slowly and effortlessly with the current, the tail of the huge mammal now and again twitching and flashing in the light. Joao followed him past, walking along the barge all the way to the stern and he kept watching till far downstream the Indian fused back into the flaming water.

From the start, Joao had said he never planned to go all the way to Cerro Verde, or even Raul. He looked only for an image to burn itself into his memory—a wedge driven between then and now. While the mine was unforgettable, it only made things worse for him; but the aboriginal clarity of the lone Indian had cured him.

They gained the outpost at Quajos early the next day. Another small, grimy barge onloaded empty fuel drums and was heading downstream later that day. While the negro and the boy rolled off most of their cargo, Joao went over and exchanged a few words with the pilot of the other barge, then returned to Paul, as usual sitting impatiently up in the bow.

"If you ever get to New York—"

"Thanks, Joao. But I don't expect I will."

"There was a time when I wished I hadn't."

"And now?"

"I doubt I'll even recognize the place."

"Look after that knee."

"I hope you find what you're looking for, Paul."

Joao moved to the mud bank as the barge pulled out into the current and started for Raul, still two days away. The deck lay bare except for several fuel drums, three pallets of various food stuffs and the ridiculous, plastic Christmas tree. Joao waved. From the bow, Paul held Joao's gaze for a long moment, smiled slightly, then turned toward the dark wilderness before him. A bend in the river, and everything behind him was gone.

Three miles upstream the river pinched and steepened into a fleet gutter of spume, keeper-holes and standing waves, and they began a tense gauntlet straight into the teeth of the creaming tide, veering around sandbars and shoals, grating over river shallows as waterlogged trees torpedoed their prow. In two weeks the returning monsoon would raise the waterline ten feet, but now in low water, they butted river boulders, battling swirling eddies to swerve back onto a precarious course. The prop got entangled in a massive clump of roots and lianas, and the negro barely throttled down before the seizing engine blew them all to Kingdom Come. As the current plowed the barge downstream and out of control, the negro dashed forward and threw off a huge anchor, which dragged and skipped along the riverbottom and finally caught with a lurch, the straining chain nearly tearing the strut off the deck; if a rusty link ever let go, the recoil would have taken someone's head clean off. The kid—a rope lashed round his waist, the negro belaying him from the helm—drew a chestful of air and dove underwater, machete in hand. Paul could hear the ticking on the prop, followed by a mass of black vines floating to the surface. Finally the kid's head burst through the foam and he gulped down half the sky in panicked mouthfuls before the current pulled him back under, and the old negro pulled harder still to reel him back into the boat. Then the anchor gave way. The kid disappeared underwater as the barge broached to the current, water gushing over the deck, and Paul scrambled back to the stern where he and the negro hauled the kid in. He collapsed on deck like a big brown fish bound in roots and creepers, hacking and wheezing with water streaming from his nose, and Paul beat on his back until he heaved and hacked some more and started breathing right. The negro slammed the old barge into gear and battled to gain an upriver line; Paul hurtled back to the bow and hand-hauled the anchor back in. On they moved, careening off rocks, grinding through snags, Paul braced in the bow, scouting and yelling out obstacles, pointing this way and that. The moment the kid caught his breath he dashed below, hammering his brains out as the old negro coaxed the rust bucket further upstream, and it went on like that the entire day.

Toward sunset the river leveled off, and on both sides the greenmetal hedgerow ran straight ahead, a magnificent hushed foyer tapering into night. The negro swung out into the middle of the sleeping river, barely 100 feet across now, and Paul threw out the anchor. A mile ahead were more cataracts, the negro said, and the three hours between them and Raul were the trickiest yet. He'd need all the daylight to navigate it. They were there, moored for the night.

Then the whole grey sky came down like a massive punch, and through the grey pane of water the land looked void and dark and without form. The deck swirled shin deep by the time the clouds ran dry ten minutes later. Throughout, Paul stood in the bow, the hot rain streaming over him, staring at the pocked water, then at the buffeting limbs of the ridiculous plastic Christmas tree, lashed to the deck. Paul had noticed the great care the negro had taken with it, never brushing its snowy limbs when off-loading drums and crates, and several times a day checking its lashings.

The new moon burned off the inky water and an electric silence fell around them. The negro gestured toward the left shore and said, "Urupa." As the two forms came into focus, Paul saw that these ghostly shapes were living things, squatting on their heels, their faces cast in irrefutable sneers. Somewhere in the bush around them lurked their clansmen, the dusky, bleeding sacrifices of an industrial juggernaut that added nothing to the beauty of their land or the life of their souls. It was a gospel of gold, all the native soil its altar stone. And seeing the quiet venom on the squatting Indians' faces, Paul understood what Orlando had seen out there that first time, and why he'd returned. For Orlando to have abandoned everything to staunch their wounds was, in Paul's eyes, what made him so terribly human and so great. He felt a tremendous release. For some time, Orlando had seemed like a man who could not possibly exist, given his long silence and nebulous letters, plus all of Joao's fears and speculations. But Paul could hear Orlando's voice again, could picture everything. He pulled out the map and added a long mark over the Rio Arce. He was drawing close.

Under a pattern of stars, the negro broke into a pallet and opened two canned hams. As Paul ate thick slices offered him on the tip of the negro's stiletto, he watched amazed as the kid devoured the entire second ham with his bare hands, glutinous, jellied fat streaming from the corners of his mouth. Then the negro found some beer and they drank three cans apiece and fell asleep where they lay.

Sunlight poured mightily over the rim of forest. Paul hauled in the anchor and they moved on through the green foyer, the engine pulsing at the same pace as his heart. Up in the highlands, it had rained most of the night. They'd seen the distant lightning, had heard the dull percussion of thunder. By morning, the river had risen above the obstacles the negro had feared upstream, and though knots of shrub and tangled branches coursed down it, the three hours to Raul passed uneventfully.

Raul. A dock of lashed tractor tires anchored to the trees. A swampy road leading to a small copper mine fourteen miles east. A cluster of drooping shacks on a rocky clearing heaped with decades of debris, great rusty mounds of it, overrun with creepers. Several denatured Indians, dressed in rags, crouched in the shadows, stranded between two worlds.

Paul found the clinic half a mile down the muddy road—tin walls, dirt floor, the smell of ammonia and tincture of benzoin so thick his eyes teared. Several men, apparently from the copper mine, were being treated for ulcerating spider bites, and a Caboclo woman looking to harbor triplets in her enormous belly lay on a table and waited silently to begin labor, her other five kids, all girls, surrounding her. The one doctor stood barely five feet tall, with sandaled feet and quick brown eyes, and he moved agilely around his cramped quarters.

His Spanish and English were not much, but with a combination of both and patois, Paul made him understand why he'd come there. "Doctor Z," the doctor said excitedly. They had worked together, in that very room. Pero hoy: Cerro Verde—eleven months—muy infermo—narcotrafficantes—worms—Indios—muchos questions. He shook his head wearily.

Quien could help him get to Cerro Verde? Paul asked.

"Nada." Only Señor Seamus used to go, but no more. "Peligroso en Cerro Verde arita," the doctor said in hack Spanish.

"How do I get there?" Paul asked in English. The doctor looked at him, nervous and annoyed, wondering just what kind of fool could fail to understand. "No passe." He put his hand on his hip, buckling at the waist to feign some imagined injury, imploring him with a stream of Portuguese Paul could not understand. Seeing none of it took, the doctor mumbled to himself, hailed a kid and sternly told him something ending with "Mister Seamus." The kid frowned, but the doctor shooed him off, pointed out Paul to the kid, and Paul followed him out, the doctor gazing after, looking like another crisis had just pulled into Raul.

After fifteen minutes slogging through dark trees they reached a small clearing beside a spring, and a matrix of shacks plaited into a central, thatched dwelling overflowing with Indian handicrafts. Paul stepped inside, squeezed past a wall of rattan baskets and into the cramped, lamp-lit space in the middle. There on the floor, in a land of ten billion trees, stood the plastic Christmas tree, and a wiry, pulled-out specimen with flame-red hair and beard. There was no flesh to the man, and Paul could see the working of his bones. His skin was so dark from tropical living that a glance would never reveal he was Anglo. Gazing up from the plastic tree, his eyes danced a little and he said, "Merry Christmas. Feliz Navidad."

"It's October," Paul said.

"Ah, English. You'd be working at the mine. A technician."

"No."

"A missionary, then. The name is Seamus, Seamus Brown, late of Gibraltar. And welcome, sir. Welcome. If you were cut from a coarser cloth we could toast your arrival—"

"I'm no missionary," Paul said. "I understand you go to Cerro Verde."

Seamus shot him a look, then quickly averted his eyes.

"I have a friend there. Doctor Orlando Zavalla." Paul added.

"Doctor Z," Seamus said softly. "A remarkable man." Seamus's blue eyes fixed Paul and he said, "You know he hiked halfway to the main fork of the Amazon inoculating Indians. That's nearly a hundred miles. Dreadful terrain. Damn near killed him getting back, it did. And they fancied the man. Maybe in the wrong way, but you can't blame them. How could any of us have really known?" Seamus said, shaking his head and staring at nothing. He seemed baffled. Something was not quite right with the redhead, thought Paul. Then he fixed on Paul again and said, "But mister, Doctor Z did get those Indians to stop killing each other. For awhile, anyway. And the missionaries never did that. No, sir. They never did. Never could." He seemed to offer these accounts as a sort of vindication—of Orlando, of himself, of the Indians for all Paul could make of it. Then as abruptly as he'd started, Seamus returned to the plastic tree.

"You've got to take me to Cerro Verde," Paul said.

Seamus quickly started arranging little seedpods on the plastic tree, fumbling, dropping several, and finally said, "Well, sir, I can't actually do that."

"Why not?"

He fiddled with the tree some more, shuffled around it to get a different perspective. "Came all the way from Brasilia and look, the snow's still on it." Seamus fingered the plastic flakes dusting the plastic limbs, and Paul noticed his hands were shaking slightly.

Paul moved between Seamus and the tree and said, "What else do you know about Doctor Zavalla?"

"Not so much."

"You're going to take me to Cerro Verde."

"Sir, I can't."

"Then rent me your boat."

"You wouldn't get a mile."

"Show me the trail."

"There is no trail."

Paul laughed angrily. He'd been in enough jungles to know the Indians always have a route to an outpost.

"You, sir, are no Indian."

Since leaving the Ranchero Zavalla, and all the way up the river, it had been pure flight for Paul, fast and mindless. Now he had to pause and face both a situation and a little of himself; both were stone walls.

They went back and forth, and every time Seamus tried to talk around the subject, Paul bore down even harder. Seamus even stumbled into the kitchen to see what liquors he had to offer by way of changing the subject altogether, but Paul wasn't buying his eccentric bit, or leaving any of it alone.

"Oh, hang it all," Seamus finally said. "Orlando and I were close friends. Yes we were."

"Were?"

"Well, we sort of fell out after things soured in Cerro Verde."

"How so?" Paul asked.

"Perhaps Doctor Z got more control over the Indians than he should have," Seamus said. "There were excesses, certainly. It went bad. But blaming someone in this place, this realm— Who's to say, really?"

"You're probably the only man who can say."

"I'm a small man, a simple man, a trader of baskets and masks," Seamus insisted. "That's all I want to be. But Dr. Z." Seamus pulled at his red beard. "I saw his weakness. I tried to save him from himself."

"What's that supposed to mean?" Paul asked.

"A man like Doctor Z, a man from the future if there ever was one—well, can't you see that kind of man just doesn't belong out here?"

The only man more puzzled than Paul was the redhead. One moment he'd seem contrite about the whole situation, then ten seconds later he'd grumble and brood like a man deceived, or betrayed, or simply ignored. It was like watching an actor who couldn't figure out his part and tried to play everything he felt, or could think of, all at once.

Paul sighed, and said, "Orlando is in Cerro Verde. That much I do know. But ever since I landed in this shit hole and started asking about him, people have been screaming at me, or jumping up and down and talking in circles, or in riddles, or not at all. And you, Mr. Brown, are going to tell me why." After a long pause, Seamus tried.

"At first I thought the doctor brought a lot to the place," Seamus said. "Now I know he brought too much."

"So you wrote him off?"

"I tried to take him down to Raul. I begged him. 'Yes, yes, we must go now,' he'd say, but he wouldn't leave and now I don't think he can. I don't know how, but something went terribly wrong, sir."

"You can leave off with the sir," Paul said, "and just tell me what went wrong?"

"I don't know, exactly." Seamus looked up from the tree, and directly at Paul. "And who really knows the man? Do you?"

"Yes."

After another hour with Seamus, Paul had squeezed out a feel for the situation, but the particulars remained as vague as Orlando's letters. After the missionaries were routed out, Seamus continued visiting Cerro Verde—to trade for native handicrafts. But shortly, the natives stopped making mats and baskets and Seamus found himself shunned, even threatened in the place he'd been going to and by the people he'd been trading with for nearly thirty years. Then, about nine months ago, Orlando had gotten sick, and word somehow leaked back to Seamus. Seamus had been run out of Cerro Verde several months before, but he went back anyway, slipped in at night, found Orlando and begged him to come back to Raul with him. He knew a bad case of gut worms was the least of Orlando's problems, for his talk was as weird and enigmatic as the natives' behavior. Seamus had to haul him out of there, for by then, as went Orlando Zavalla de Fonseca, so would go Cerro Verde and everyone in it. Orlando refused to leave and, in a moment of raw candor, made Seamus promise him to never come back to Cerro Verde, as the situation had taken on a momentum all its own and nobody was safe any-more. Yet Seamus again returned, hoping the doctor in the clinic could reason with Orlando. They were stopped some ways up the river, the doctor taking an arrow in the hip. And that was the last of it, over eight months ago.

They'd tried to reel him back in, but they'd lost him. Orlando was gone, and Cerro Verde effectively sealed off. Now, in Raul, they heard only random rumors and wild talk that might as well have come from Uranus, for the fifty miles separating him from Cerro Verde was like an infinity. Seamus was convinced that to go anywhere near there would bring on trouble he doubted they could handle. Then strangely, he started in with his own ques-tions, as though Paul might supply the missing pieces of a prodi-gious puzzle.

Paul started with Orlando at the University, at the Ranchero Zavalla, on the beach in Morocoy, trying to make Seamus believe he was the one man Orlando would never refuse. Seamus assured him that the man Paul had revered in the Zavalla library, the man Seamus had revered in that very dwelling, was no longer the same as the man holed up on the Bolivian border, fifty miles upstream. Of course, Orlando would cut a remarkable pose against a background of wood and water, Paul argued, so no wonder there'd been some small confusion, what with all the flakes and religious tyrants vying for the natives' regard. Who would they gravitate toward, and who could fault their choice? They were not the first.

"Orlando wants to run things his own way," Paul said, "more power to him."

"Too much power," Seamus said.

Paul would consider—though not admit—that Orlando had changed, and that perhaps Orlando would even refuse him; but he would never harm him, or anyone with him, no matter the changes of the one or the fallout with the other.

"I might as well be the man's brother," Paul said.

And so Paul convinced Seamus to send a local Indian up toward Cerro Verde with word that they were coming. If

Orlando objected, the Indians could turn them back on the river. Local Indians were of a different tribe than those upstream who had stopped coming to Raul nearly a year back, but a local could get the word out.

The river twisted through the contours of a low canyon. To the left and to the right, before and behind, rolling, mounting, sinking, rising, like swells in a huge green sea, was the jungle. The canyon walls suddenly reared, and they rattled on, deep into the green void. Since leaving Raul, it had rained continuously—not an honest rain, but a galling, pissy little drizzle.

Seamus' small canoe, hewn from the trunk of a ramin tree and shored up with hardwood spars, ran gunnel high with food, trade goods, tools and spare parts for the inevitable breakdowns. Clamped to the square stern whined a forty-horsepower outboard motor. In shallow water, Seamus would quickly hinge it up out of the river to keep from shearing the prop pin or even losing a blade to the rocks. He knew the river, which in only five miles had narrowed and presently surged through shallow rocky furrows, the canoe grating past these bottlenecks, sometimes checked dead in the current, standing waves pouring over the bow. The engine would scream away, cavitating in the spume as Seamus jockeyed the engine's pitch. Paul poled in the bow, pressing his weight over a long staff which scatted on the shifting river bottom to finally get a moment's purchase, causing the canoe to lurch forward: Paul would tumble back, snatch the bucket and start furious bailing before they shot another gap.

Seamus carried on with no thrill of adventure, rather with the gloomy perception of hazard and the dark relationships of strange events upriver. Yet he still clung to a sliver of hope that things were somehow different than he thought. And he continually babbled, though not necessarily to Paul, for he'd acquired the sketchy practice of thinking out loud to calm his nerves, addressing himself here in reverential tones, there in rhymes, other times scolding himself like a child for hitting rocks or running aground. When they ground over a sharp rib of rock, water spewed through a rent in the hull and they barely made the shore before they swamped.

They emptied the canoe onto a pebbly spit, flipped it over and Seamus began stuffing strips of burlap into a thin, yard-long crack that ran with the grain of the wood. Then he hammered the strips deep into the crack with a ball-peen hammer and a screwdriver, all the while babbling. He had not blundered into his life there. He had his wife to thank for it—"A fine, upright woman." After she left him, he searched his store for the one thing he thought he couldn't live without: a basket, a black leopard artfully woven into the pear-shaped form, very rare and fashioned by the natives upriver. He left his family's import shop in Gibraltar the next week. That happened twenty-eight years ago, and he hadn't been back since. Just sent things off every four months to an agent in São Paulo.

As Seamus thumbed a gummy resin over the crack, Paul wondered why he'd agreed to take him to Cerro Verde. Or to try to. Sooner than later, Seamus would have to start trading with the Indians again or he'd go bust. Or maybe he was simply curious, or felt loyalties to the man he had defended and begged downstream but who'd run him out. Maybe Seamus felt guilty himself. Or perhaps he got carried along by Paul's drive, even though Paul's arguments about his and Orlando's friendship had been as unconvincing as his promise of their safe passage to a land he'd never been to and whose people he'd never seen. No telling, Paul thought. Seamus hadn't really said, and Paul wasn't going to start asking now.

Seamus made a torch from a rag and a shank of bamboo, and for half an hour he moved the low flame over the resin he'd thumbed into the crack in the canoe until it set hard as glass. Then he filed the repair flush to the hull and they flipped the canoe back over, loaded it up, pushed out into the river and motored on.

The first night they slept on a sandbar beneath the overturned canoe. The second and third nights, they pitched hammocks in the jungle, the disposition of the unseen locals weighing heavily on Seamus' mind. They'd seen signs—a few campfires, and fleeting shadows between the thinning trees. Then, that afternoon, they'd passed two Indians, squat and feral, peering down from a calving mud buttress above the narrowing river. But the Indians made no gesture or greeting, simply watched them crawl past.

It was well into the night, but neither man could win sleep. A hole in the green canopy framed the crescent moon, a lone star at its edge.

"You don't need imagination out here," Seamus said, swinging in his hammock. "You need restraint."

"Otherwise you start ordering plastic Christmas trees and yakking to yourself?" Paul asked.

Seamus chuckled and said, "If a person's lucky, or a fool, he'll stop there." Seamus had stopped there, but not from luck or foolishness. He had twenty-eight years in this realm, enough to know that the basic conditions of human life were precisely those of nature, and that immutable natural forces were ignored, or commandeered, only at great personal peril—a crucial bit of wisdom remarkably lost on Orlando. "He wanted it all, for himself, and his own way," Seamus said, shaking his head.

He described his first encounters with Orlando, whose aspiring excellence had captured him. So this was the modern man, Seamus recalled thinking. He seemed far beyond what had ever arrived in the Amazon—beyond the grasping garimpeiros and thieving military, beyond all the petty spiritual monarchs, and by his own admission beyond all their timid faith—and it struck Seamus as the freshest breeze. He'd taken Orlando to Cerro Verde when the French doctor needed help. For years, the missionaries had called the tune in Cerro Verde, allowing no variations on the theme; but Orlando played a very different opus and when the new missionaries were forced out and Orlando stayed on, Seamus had high hopes for better trade and better relations with the tribesmen. Yet suddenly and inexplicably Orlando took on a grim tone with no likeness to the original and no concern for anything but his extemporized designs.

"God knows what set him off," Seamus said. "Maybe the isolation, or the freedom. Probably the freedom. This place can grab a man's weakness and run wild with it, because there's no restraints beyond your own basic stuff, and nothing to stop the maddest ambitions but madness itself."

"What do you actually know?" Paul asked.

"How much can you know, fifty miles away?"

"Nothing for certain, I should think."

"I hope I'm wrong about it all," Seamus said. "But I do know he and his loyalists controlled the river and all the people on it, all the way into Bolivia. And that some months ago, the whole area got so hot that even the narcotrafficantes were driven off and now wouldn't go anywhere near Cerro Verde."

The river got rockier and narrower and they had to portage so many stretches it struck Paul that they were trying to reach Cerro Verde with the canoe on their backs. Humping the outboard engine was enormous labor, the canoe more so. They kept having to shag back and forth for the food and gas and trade goods, load back up, motor for a mile—at the most—then portage all over again. The remains of old splintered dugouts resting high up on the gnarled shore said theirs was the only course, though. Finally, the river leveled off and the rain returned in earnest. They put back in and motored into a gorge formed by steep mud slabs that rose directly from the river and bore water striations fifteen feet above the present waterline. Seamus anxiously powered on through the fleet but level current, Paul bailing three bucketfuls a minute. After two hours the river started surging. Quantities of mud and debris washed past them, and on the black walls of the gorge Paul could see the river rising by the second.

"We've got to find a clearing," Seamus yelled through the pounding rain and the din of the screaming outboard, his eyes scanning both walls of the muddy bastille. From the waterline, the dirt walls stretched upward at a forty-five-degree angle to a fringe of verdure high overhead. There were no breaks, no side canyons. They had to get off the river, yet all they could do was to keep on, trapped in a culvert boiling and rising a foot a minute.

Then the terrain grew strange and almost formless, the mud slabs giving way to conglomerate stone riven with spontaneous side creeks completely flooded and pumping into the river, which suddenly converged into a bottleneck barely twenty yards wide and chocked with uprooted trees and bush. The flood behind spewed thirty-foot brown geysers through rifts in the jetsam dam grinding and shifting in the breech, the pressure so great that enormous logs were twisting like corkscrews and snapping with the concussion of cannon fire. Seamus frantically cranked over to a fluted section of the tapered slot and the two men groped onto sloping, mossy rock, hauling and shoving the canoe over a slanting stone bench swirling and knee deep, streams of dark slosh pouring off awnings of rock and into their canoe. They shoved and heaved until their hands were striped with blood blisters and their ankles twisted and their knees raw from barking the rock, but they'd gotten the canoe above the logjam and into a seething lagoon that overflowed a hundred yards into bordering forest. Seamus tied off the canoe to a tree and, peering out through a mask of brown slop, said, "Sir, that's as close as it gets."

Both men moved to higher ground, commanding a view of the grinding bottleneck and the dam of trees that finally let go, disgorging a great muddy wave down the river, sloshing far up the muddy walls containing it. The huge brown breaker tore around a corner and just as suddenly, the swirling lagoon settled and sank as though someone had pulled a giant plug from the river bottom, water from the flanking forest draining quickly down and bringing with it more trees and brush, which flowed straight into the bottleneck and clogged the slot and the lagoon started backing up again.

Their canoe now aground, Seamus and Paul pushed it through a shoal of silt and into the rising lagoon and motored away. They'd finally reached the highlands, a strange blend of alpine and forest habitats, as though nature couldn't decide which realm it preferred, and took on aspects of both. The jungle thinned out, the trees were less bunched and the ground beneath them littered with fractured schist. The overhead canopy had opened up, exposing a slate grey sky and the air was pure and cool. The river was narrower still, but flat and slow moving.

Soon, tall, mottled boulders, eroded at the base, rose from the current like great tenpins on end. Some miles in the distance, outlined one against the other, the crests of a low cordillera seemed shuffled like a deck of stony cards—brusque peaks, bluish draws, jutting arêtes swaying and rising and falling in the harsh light. Then the sun dipped down and the stars rushed out and they had to pull over only a couple miles short of Cerro Verde. After all those days bashing up the river, Paul was vexed to get stopped so close, and spent an hour pacing the riverbank. No one could navigate that rock-strewn river in even the sharpest moonshine, and for a stranger to trek into a remote place in the middle of the night seemed too dicey even for Paul to consider. He finally stopped pacing when he realized the one good sign: They'd been seen. All of Cerro Verde knew they were coming, and as yet they hadn't been warned or driven off.

Seamus deftly made a circular cut around the base of a sapling, then a second cut a yard higher, pried the bark back from the lower cut and wiggled off a hollow tube of pliable stuff. A swift trip through a copse of bamboo and he had flooring and joist for a slick lean-to that he expertly lashed together with lianas, roofed with palm fronds and floored with the supple bark. The man's speed and dexterity equaled that of any native Paul had ever seen, and snug in their waterproof shelter, Paul asked, "So Seamus, how's your trade with the Indians been these last months?"

"Not much, I'm afraid."

"You had a pretty fair store of goods at your place in Raul."

"Fair, yes."

"I'm thinking a man skilled as you are probably knows something about making native stuff, pretty much just like the natives make it."

"I know a thing or two."

"I bet a crafty man—if he were pressed into it—might make the stuff himself, and hawk it as the real thing."

"If he were pressed into it, perhaps he would."

"So, this last year, say, how much of the Indian crafts coming out of Raul have been your handiwork?"

"Some of it, anyway."

"How much, Seamus?"

"All of it," he mumbled after a pause.

"And what you've been telling me about Orlando—how much of that is as phony as the baskets you've been shipping to São Paulo?"

"What kind of crazy question is that?" Seamus asked, snapping up and glaring at Paul.

"No less crazy than the swill you've been feeding me about Orlando, I figure."

"You figure wrong, sir." Seamus huffed and fumed for a moment and asked, "And just why would I want to go and make it all up?"

"A new man shows up with his own ideas—some people are going to try and make him fail."

"Some people might."

"I met a missionary a couple weeks ago who nearly bit my head off just mentioning Orlando's name."

Seamus pulled at his beard in anger and amazement.

"Look here, Paul, the questions you have are the same ones I have myself, so you can't expect me to have the answers. But understand that I believed in Doctor Z, see? Truly I did. And there's no man alive who'd rather find out that all the talk is bloody rubbish. When you arrived, I decided it was time to find out, one way or the other."

"And you will," Paul said.

◆ ◆ ◆

Seamus pulled the canoe over short of the rough water at the confluence. Just ahead, the Rio Arce was barely twenty yards wide as it spilled from a larger river that flowed east and disappeared into a narrow, steamy canyon rumbling with cataracts. A footpath led away from the fork of the two rivers; Paul hit it at speed, leaving Seamus to look after the canoe. Seamus' nerve had started going that morning. He was ruined by the time they reached the fork. Paul figured the second he vanished down the trail, Seamus would blast for home and wouldn't ease off the throttle till he was hanging seedpods on the plastic Christmas tree.

A half mile along the trail and the trees fell away, revealing a low, jagged rib of peaks. After the long claustrophobia of the river passage, this modest range seemed mighty as the Andes; yet it was utterly shamed by a colossal spire, blanketed in purple moss and ferns and dangling vines, firing off the lower massif like a great emerald bullet, reaching, tapering, till its needle-thin crown finally shot into a cloud a thousand feet above. Though never in his life had he been in such a hurry, the first sight of that spire stopped Paul in his steps. It was Cerro Verde, the Green Peak, and he could imagine no massif on earth bearing a more imposing sentinel. He pressed on.

The whole area held a funereal silence, the few slender trees standing in disbelief against a backdrop of grey rock and olive scrub. When Paul finally spotted the cluster of old missionary structures, his stomach knotted tight. He walked into the first structure to find a woman bandaging a young Indian boy's hand. She glanced up and froze like a deer caught in headlights. A mestiza, she had a plain face and a plain blue cotton dress, worn thin about the shoulders from countless scrubbings on the river stones. A nurse or a medic, Paul thought to himself. Whatever, for certain she was no Indian and was the last thing Paul expected to find there. The strength of the wilderness seemed concentrated in her eyes.

"Who are you?" Paul asked in English.

"Como?" she asked. Her voice didn't betray any concern. And in her one word, Paul caught the Bolivian accent.

"Who are you?" he asked in Spanish.

"Who are you?" she asked right back.

Only then did Paul realize how conned he'd been by the rumors. The woman's very presence there refuted them all.

"I've come to see Doctor Zavalla," he said.

The young Indian boy glanced up at Paul and said, "Muerto."
"Dead?" Paul blared out.

Ever calm, the woman asked the boy if he was sure. He said no, he wasn't sure, though for some days now all the people had been waiting for the doctor to die. Eying the stranger, the woman said she had arrived in Cerro Verde only two weeks before, and had never actually seen the doctor. And the Indians were not talking.

"Where is the doctor?" Paul asked.

"So far as I know he's in the old missionary's home," the woman said.

The boy nodded; but when Paul asked where it was she shook her head and said it was an Indian problem and that, for his own safety, Paul ought to quickly return from wherever he had come and she was too busy to start worrying about a stranger and so forth.

"Just tell me where the missionary's house is, señorita, and I'll do the worrying."

The woman's black eyes narrowed, and looking straight at Paul she curtly told the boy to guide the stranger to the old missionary's dwelling.

All the way across a splintered granite intrusion, Paul wondered why the house lay so far from the clinic. Then the boy stopped and pointed the way, and Paul charged on, stopping only at a circle of charcoal—burnt limbs and sticks—ringing the small dwelling. Whatever it meant, it was a recent statement, for the hourly rains had barely doused it. Paul stepped over the charred ring and almost choked on the hot copper taste rushing into his mouth and down his throat. He turned from the house. The boy had gone. There was no one around, none to be seen anyway; and now, more than then, Paul felt the eyes of a hundred silent watchers pressing on him. Their hiding was plain as bad news ever got.

Paul turned back to the house. It had one glass window, covered from the inside, which God himself must have delivered there in one piece. Next to it was a plank door. Paul moved to it, knocked, and after getting no answer pushed his way inside and over the frontier of his world.

The stench of waste and sickness and tart acrid smoke hit Paul like a fist. A faint glow bled through the mat over the window, otherwise it was totally dark inside. A solitary horsefly buzzed through the close air. Slowly, his eyes adjusted, and Paul could just make out a shadowy form on the cane bed.

"Orlando?" Paul asked. "Orlando."

The body shifted slightly on the bare mattress. Paul moved to the window and threw back the matt: the body reeled from the light, shriveled into a ball and screamed, "Oh, Jesus. Close that."

The savage fact of that cringing wreck, naked, fouled, lank greasy hair falling over his bony shoulders, pasty white skin clinging to a rack of ribs, crushed Paul like an avalanche of rock and ice. A man lay there, yet so loathsome and debased he could not possibly be alive, and didn't seem to be but for the yellow fire his eyes flashed back in the light.

"The light. Get rid of the light," he begged.

Paul pulled the mat most of the way over the window, though a little sun still washed over Orlando's body from about the waist down, showing his scaly legs, pocked with weeping boils. Paul noticed the small clay pipe clutched in his fist, and that the mattress was littered with stick matches and several dishes of wax or some kind of paste. It could have been an hour or a minute before Orlando finally spoke.

"Did you come in from Raul, or Bolivia?" His voice sounded even, but the promise Paul had hauled all the way up the river had died so fast and so ignobly that it was an age before he could mutter, "From Raul."

"Then you came up with Seamus. He knows these people well. He knows the river better."

He thumbed a dab of paste into his pipe, struck a match, waved the flame over the bowl and drew hard. His yellow eyes bulged, then foundered in his skull as the coca paste gurgled in the pipe and the smoke gurgled in his lungs. When he finally wheezed out a cloud, he melted back on the bed and his limbs started ticking, the light cutting across his heaving ribs. The smoke hung there like slow death and watered Paul's eyes. He doubted Orlando even knew who he was speaking to, his voice sounded so far away.

"Have you ever seen a jacaranda tree? They have a straight white trunk and the crown, when it blooms, is purple, and sometimes even blue. They're the forest's most miraculous statement, each one a miracle. You never see two at a time because they're so few. They always stand alone. When I was hiking back from Yano Mani territories, I saw the greatest jacaranda in Brazil. It must have been incredible in its day. It's dead now. The jungle. Strangler figs were coiled round the white trunk—squeezed the spirit out of it. The crown was bald and black and even the birds wouldn't roost in it."

He rambled on and on. It may have been Orlando's finest hour, but Paul didn't hear a word, each meaning, every passage fading into the other. The voice, a sputtering monotone from the other side, heaped Paul, stunned him, clenched him. It had already ripped his heart out; now it clawed after his soul. Orlando grabbed another stick match, but paused and struggled up onto both elbows, his face still in the greyness.

"Before we were born, this place was waiting for us. Our whole existence has led us here, to show us The Fact that every path leads into this eternity which leads nowhere." His thin, jittery hand reached out and carved the light below his ribs. "Answers?" he said, and his coughing seemed to have a strain of laughter in it. "Only half answers, partial answers, each one uncovering another question. No, the only thing we really have is The Fact. No one wants to hear it, so they'll saw and chop and burn it up but The Fact will still scream at us from the ashes. It endures; but you and I, Juancho, must die."

The mention of his name wrenched Paul from the grip of that room, that savaged shell. He went over to the window and ripped off the mat: light flooded in and Orlando shrieked, but Paul just stared at him, shivering on the mattress. Orlando rolled his head away from the light. It was a younger part of him that finally spoke, lonesome and disbelieving.

Dying had become a terrible ordeal, he said. He'd courted it, borrowed its authority, watched death as death might watch itself. He had put in months of hard work, and all his concentration and energy chasing it. But it eluded him. Now holed up and circled in, he'd fasted for days, sucking on that pipe till hell wouldn't have it any more, yet he still couldn't die. It seemed the harder he pursued it, the more patient and invincible death became.

Paul said nothing, and turned to leave.

"Who are you to judge me?" Orlando screamed.

Paul wheeled at the door. "Who do I have to be?"

"You'd have to understand The Fact. It's impossible to know what is necessary if you don't." Orlando turned his cadaverous face into the light. "We are eaten by fury and hatred. By hope. By love eaten. But we're all dead men conversing with the dead."

Paul wanted to scream: "No shit, you goddam fool." But there wasn't enough there to scream at or pray for, not enough to even haul back down the river. There was nothing on that mattress but soul-madness and malevolence.

Orlando sighed, leaned back on the bed and asked, "What did you expect to find here, Juancho?"

"Orlando Zavalla de Fonseca. Not you."

Orlando coughed out a little laugh, and in a final burst of sincerity said, "You know I was always jealous of you, because I saw in you what I could never have. But you'll never find it because you don't know what it is, don't even know you have it." That magnificent ruin had pronounced his last judgement, no less strange and bewildering than the rest that he had said. He'd always had the ability to glimpse a truth and draw it out of people, a knack that destroyed him when he turned it on himself. With great effort Orlando bent his head into the light, and again in a voice reaching back to when they were both much younger, he softly said, "I envy your grief, Juancho. Envy your grief."

He fingered a big dollop of paste into his pipe and stoked it with a match. The paste crackled and billowed as he huffed hard, the yellow flame highlighted his yellow cheeks sinking in and his thin yellow skin tightened on his face, describing a perfect skull, better than dead and yet repulsively, unthinkably alive, mocking life, hope, love. He kept drawing on that pipe till his last nerve fired off. Then he fell back, out cold.

Paul went over and felt the weak, racing pulse. His ordeal was almost over. What would Doña Dometilda ever think, Paul wondered, if she knew just how far from the Ranchero Zavalla her son had really gone. He'd turned from them. Then he'd turned from himself. He hated it all, and now he struggled to die as the scorpion stings itself. Even death didn't want him now. Paul had never seen a man so broken up and ripped apart.

Paul staggered back to the clinic and found Seamus there talking to the Bolivian nurse and an Indian man Seamus had known for twenty years, and who had been one of Orlando's guides on his fated march back from Yano Mani territories. Trying to dig up an explanation for the human offal he'd just left was Paul's sudden obligation, for he had nowhere to go and nothing to do—for the rest of his natural life—and the gloom of this predicament was too great to imagine or even consider. So he began his inquisition, as though it were the most important thing he would ever do.

The Bolivian nurse knew little. The Indian knew a lot, as did a Urupa concubine Orlando had taken early on. She was called to the clinic and turned up with a few letters which, luckily, never made it out to Orlando's mother. Paul had barely made it through the letters when other Indians started trickling in; and within minutes, the place overflowed with natives who found a chance to publicly vent their shame and outrage. They went on for hours, in half a dozen different tongues, sometimes wailing, often screaming over each other. When several of the more outrageous storytellers started repeating themselves, the crowd began to thin. By early afternoon only Paul, Seamus, and the Boliviana were left to sift through it all and piece together a scenario of the annihilation of Orlando Zavalla de Fonseca.

All had been well when Orlando trekked off north for Yano Mani territories on a polio vaccine junket the French doctor had always planned but lacked the youth and dash to ever pull off. The junket proved an adventure and a success. But everything changed getting back to Cerro Verde. Orlando and his two Indian guides were seven days thrashing cross-country to avoid warring natives, and found themselves forced onto high ground, away from the streams. It never rained. Their tongues turned black and they would have drunk their own urine if they'd had any. On the night of the fifth day without water, racked by hallucinations, Orlando stared into the abyss and saw only The Fact—that he counted for nothing against natural forces totally indifferent to individual existence. All his poetry and logic and aristocratic hauteur seemed as slight and, fundamentally, as meaningless as the desperate trek that had led him there. He could not best this abyss. He could not change it. "It didn't care," he wrote in one of the letters. "It was annihilation writ large: a river of lava, a plague, a cataclysm, me but a body entombed in molten rock, a rotting corpse, another random life thrown into the hole. And looming huge before me, it set me at naught, slaying who I thought I was."

Other men had seen the rocks spit and the graves open, had heard the voice, nameless and malignant, cry out: Cast thyself down. And yet some had turned away to do great things with their numbered days. But these men had had a trust, a faith, however small, with which to defy the voice. Orlando, Paul knew, had only his native genius and a savage self-conceit.

Had Orlando been in a brisk city, at the Ranchero Zavalla, even with Paul, he might have parried his reflections and marched straight through the vale of tears. But stranded at the last place on no map, the abyss slowly closed around him, seemed everywhere, became everything, and his decaying genius was no proof against its power. For a time he found "the strength and clarity necessary to walk the jagged edge of The Fact," as he'd said in his earlier letter, for he remained a man of enormous inner strength. But like a climber clinging to the high crag who has suddenly run out of holds, little by little, his resolve, his esteem and finally his desire flaked off like shale; and Orlando Zavalla de Fonseca cast himself in. He fell, screaming through a sheer dark void at the center of himself. Two days later, he fell out the other side.

His world upended, his passions now flowed south to north. He did not simply forget who he had been, rather he energetically loathed that image, countering all that he once stood for with fire and depravity. He embraced The Fact, and called that courage. He adopted its own methods, became the first son of Mars, beyond all judgement. He had, in fact, gone mad, and quickly set a course to make all Cerro Verde converse with the dead.

He orchestrated the missionaries' demise, then took on the aspect of a wily shaman, with potions and needles and the dazzling, impenetrable talk of the gods. His miraculous cures and natural canniness won him the blind and savage loyalty of the simple forest people, whose children he then sold into slavery at jungle drug labs. He forced chiefs and elders to paddle kilos of cocaine downstream to government officials who half the time shot them dead upon delivery. It was also said he'd killed and eaten seven narcotrafficantes and had sodomized the devil and that he cast a shadow only under a full moon. Before the crowd in the clinic had broken up, the stories had gotten progressively more and more excessive until nobody could separate the lies from the facts, and Paul knew the useful details were behind them now.

Seamus, who knew a smattering of many native tongues and was accustomed to weeding through the embroidered way most

Indians related "information," was indispensable in reckoning the uneven testimonies. Her two weeks in Cerro Verde had only obscured the whole business for the Bolivian nurse, and she could offer little. Strictly speaking, the clinic was in Bolivia, and hearing that the missionaries had been driven out, she, a junior health worker, was dispatched to establish a Bolivian presence. Actually, the whole works was tied up with the Bolivian cocaine trade, which as usual, the army controlled. But the nurse knew nothing of it, and her courage seemed great, sublime, having lasted even these two weeks with such stress in the air.

Late that afternoon, Paul and Seamus went back to the old missionary house and found Orlando dead. Just as Paul began wrapping the body in a sheet, Seamus let out a yell and a black worm the size of a garter snake crept from Orlando's mouth.

"We've got to get him in the ground," Paul said.

"He's got to be burned," Seamus said. The Indians all said so. They'd planned it for two weeks. The pit had been dug, the pyre gathered. Paul cradled Orlando in his arms and outside, the two men were met by several Indians who led them to a distant knoll, and Paul set the body on the pyre of bamboo and cane that went ten feet deep into the ground. Indians from seven tribes surrounded the blaze which shot cinders high into the deep blue night and flashed across the weary faces of human beings utterly surfeited with abuse and death. But as the biting reek of burning flesh rose from the pit, so rose the Indians' spirits. It was a great moment of celebration and dirges and jeers and wailing, for the white devil-god was burning and the people were their own masters again.

In an hour, Orlando Zavalla de Fonseca was only so many ashes in a deep red pit. The Indians threw in handfuls of dirt until the hole was flush with the ground and all that remained was a tendril of white steam hissing from the soil. Paul tried to imagine Orlando now, mingling with the coals, the clayey earth. He remembered the elegant care Orlando had always paid his person—the long saunas, the rub-downs, the Parisian hair oils and genuine colognes, the ivory linen suits. He couldn't believe Orlando had come to this.

The next morning, Paul and Seamus walked along the river in the shade of Cerro Verde. Seamus had left all his trade goods at the clinic, and would return to Raul for more. The Indians were still celebrating, but it would take some doing to regain their confidence. Neither man mentioned Orlando, though his presence hung like millstones on them both.

Directly beneath the towering green spire, Seamus stopped at a large cairn of red rocks and an old, flimsy dugout tied to the shore. The rocks were a monument to a Urupa myth as old as Cerro Verde: that anyone who willfully paddled a canoe into the roaring canyon below would live forever. Or maybe the rocks were in honor of the warrior said to have done the crazy thing. Seamus didn't know the fine points. The canoe was there for anyone who should want to find out for themselves, though it was mostly to keep the wonderful myth alive. Twenty years of missionaries had tried to destroy it, but never could. If that canoe had anyone's name on it, Paul thought, it was Orlando Zavalla de Fonseca's. It was a journey he should have taken.

"You going to be able to get your canoe back down the river by yourself?" Paul asked.

"Been doing it twenty-eight years," Seamus said. "So you're staying?"

"For now."

For three days, Paul stayed in a small, dirt-floored room adjoining the clinic, and for three days the Boliviana wondered who he was and what he was doing or planned to do. Not until after Seamus had left and he laid back on the cot did Paul realize just how wasted he'd become. Yet he couldn't sleep. He just lay there in limbo, with nowhere to go and no angle off that cot. Now, he had to start his own ordeal. In fact, it had already started, with a slight numbness in his side and a whiteness under his fingernails.

Dreadful moaning from the clinic had seeped through the walls for several hours, and finally Paul could bear it no longer. He got up and stumbled down to the river and sat back on the shore. The moon had started to walk on the sleeping river, and for a long hour he lay back and looked up at the cobalt sky and recalled the only poem he really knew—how everywhere the blue sky belongs to the stars, and is their native country and their appointed rest, which they enter unannounced; and how as lords they are certainly expected and yet there is silent joy at their arrival. If only he could go there on a rocket, he thought, a rocket that would never come down. But the closer he looked, the more he realized how cold and distant they all seemed, and bitterly comparing their desolation to his own, he turned and started back to the room.

Then he stopped.

What was this maudlin crap? he asked himself. Christ! He'd been trying to sing a ballad to a head-on collision. Then he started laughing, but not really laughing, nor crying—rather a bottomless, baffled noise that told what a farce it had all been. What a pointless, existential fraud. And the notion that he could construct his own history, could alter the fate stamped on his forehead at birth was the biggest lie of them all. He didn't even have the satisfaction of having made his own mistakes. They all just happened, right on the heels of each other, like falling dominos. Who could fathom it? Why did Orlando even bother? Paul Hudson didn't give a damn about anything anymore—until he got back to his room, which was not even his room.

Everyone has something they will not let others touch; and the Boliviana, sitting on the cot in Paul's room, the document tube at her side, had the very article—Paul's diploma from medical school—in her hands. She looked up and said, "I knew you were a doctor. I knew this."

Paul snatched his diploma, and quickly stuffing it back into the tube, said, "You had no right to search my belongings."

"And you had no right to lie in here while I struggled with the sick ones. I'm not even a proper nurse."

"And I'm not a proper doctor. I never even finished my residency."

She laughed. "You think anyone here cares? Caramba. Why are you still here?"

"I'm here to die."

She looked at Paul for a moment and said, "I am not impressed that you come here to die. I think you have already died."

Paul glared at her. "Doctor Zavalla. If you could have only known him before, maybe you'd understand."

"It's dangerous to try and make a man in your own image."

"My image wasn't that wreck I burned three days ago."

"Well, what are you going to do now?" she said without pausing. "What?"

He went into the clinic, got a lantern and walked over to the missionary's house.

Paul had no idea what he hoped to find. The shabby little dwelling had little in it. Just the bed, a few clothes and a green ammo can. Seamus had chucked all the drug garbage and swept the place out before he'd left. Paul sat back on the bed and played back that last bit Orlando said, about the vague substance he was said to have but would never find—a remark he'd passed over in silence for a number of reasons. What the hell was Orlando talking about? He pushed the question through every portal of his mind and through his chest and down his arms and under his white fingernails, but for the dwindling life inside him, he couldn't find a flashpoint, couldn't reckon what it could be. Some secret knowledge? Some answer. Some innate concern? Of death? So he'd die. The farce is over. He was way past fear now, past the world; and Orlando was past everything. He shouldn't have been jealous.

Almost as an afterthought, Paul went over and opened up the ammo can. Inside were three small gold bars. He slowly grabbed one in each hand, held them up to the lantern and stared at them. The bars were brilliant light amber, yet so covered with carnage that they seemed to throb red as a jagged wound, each bar a symbol of the greed and madness for power that through the years had made cutthroats of generals, and kings out of cut-throats. All the way up the river he had seen the eternal curse, more naked and certain than he could ever have seen it in Slade, Montana, or Caracas or New York. All the divers and sifters and soldiers and doctors, as though overrunning an old rust bucket clanking up a river that would never end. On deck raged the savage battle, each band, every man slashing and clawing over the stairs and each other to lay hold of the helm and set the course. And all these would-be captains knew the same thing. Nothing. Not the fatal currents, nor the soul of the land, nor yet the people who lived there. They never steered with clear reason, rather on impulse and gut lust, salting the wake with the defeated; and when the engine faltered or their course strayed, they too were pitched overboard by the stronger, the fiercer. And the barge would forge on—for gold, for a kingdom, for the third stone from the sun and everyone on it—till the greed and cruelty had bled out of every living thing. And when that time came, Paul thought, perhaps even the gold, and the memory of Orlando Zavalla de Fonseca, would be washed clean again. But he would not be there to see it.

Then a glacial sweat washed over him and he could feel the shadow of death leering over his shoulder. It had been there since the first lash of his stepfather's belt. His indomitable drive had always kept him one step ahead of it because the hope that he could do something in this world—no matter how little he understood it or how little it wanted him—was all that sustained him. In the very room where his drive had expired, his shadow had finally caught him. He would never create anything now, would never move things along, would never know the satisfaction of having done anything while hanging on in this fractured world. He would simply die, without leaving so much as a single pylon in the mud to show for all his suffering.

His stepfather was dead. Trevor Novak was dead. They all were dead, or so far away as to be dead. He lay back on the mattress that Doctor Orlando Zavalla de Fonseca had slain himself on and his limbs slowly enfolded on themselves till he was drawn up in a tight fetal knot, shaking and sweating. Finally, thinking only of a flimsy canoe tied to a rock in the shadow of a great green spire, Paul Hudson passed out.

◆ ◆ ◆

That she would so figure in the closing months of Paul Hudson's history was lost on him for weeks, weeks that later he wished he could have back. Rifling through his belongings was only the start of it. She rifled through him from head to foot, tossing the deadstanding and snatching out and holding to light those splinters of character that endured in spite of the external conditions that had gutted the rest of him. It was always—Why do you feel like this? Will you help me here? What are you going to do? And when? And throughout he had the irksome feeling that she knew the answer to every question she asked. So beaten down and routed was he that the whole business drove him crazy—none of it so much as getting blindsided and unmasked, shown over and over that he didn't know who he was or what he needed. He felt chilly and naked so for some weeks he just went through the motions, glad only that he had something to beguile his days away. He'd written off the idea of creating anything in this world, but she pushed at his blind spot even harder. With as little time as they had left together, she had to work fast.

Her name was Rafaella Camille Falcon, a nurse's aide from a blighted patch of chaparral in northeastern Bolivia. She was plain as the rain was wet, but she put all of herself into her work, and was the first reason the Indians started coming back to the clinic. It took time, and all her many devices, before Paul quit cringing at himself and accepted her challenge to give up to his vocation at the last place on no map. It held the promise of something vague; and only after three months, after Paul had lost twenty-five pounds and could sleep only four hours a night, after the two of them had endured many failures—including a wave of cholera that took seven people in three days—did the picture come into focus for Doctor Paul Hudson.

He had barely been aware of the little kindnesses she performed for him, or that he'd come to expect. Yet as the weeks went by, and he woke in the morning, the thought of her made him anxious to be up and in the clinic. Then one night, when his feet felt like blocks of ice and his guts wouldn't stop burning, he found himself wandering through the little clinic, empty for the first time in weeks. He lighted one of the lamps. Looking around at the wooden tables and the tamped dirt floor and the many other reminders of the hours he'd spent in this room, he understood what pure therapy it had all been for him. But it was the silence, the complete stillness in the room that made him understand that therapy alone had not healed his spirit.

He sat down on a wooden bench and went back to the man who had charged into Cerro Verde so few months before, a desperate, self-loathing man locked into a kind of all-encompassing selfishness. His own shadows had roped him into a no-man's-land in which he could not see and could not feel anything but the distortions of his own existence. He'd gambled as only a hopeless man can gamble, and had chased after Orlando not so much for the reasons he had told himself, but because flight, especially dangerous flight, gave him a mission and a means to run away from himself. But Paul could not outrun himself, and Orlando's sagest words had plunged him below zero. All the genius in all the world could not have saved either one of them. But inside that clinic, Paul's smallest gesture came to give off a spark that could light the eyes of an old Indian doomed to cholera and redeem a young doctor sentenced to leukemia. Nothing human was really possible and nothing at all was tolerable without that spark. And if his life was the price he had paid to get it, even then he knew that the smallest bit of human kindness was worth everything.

Paul went to Rafaella's room, and leaned against the threshold. "I can probably steal another couple months."

While he'd always figured God never had much use for him, Rafaella certainly did. She shifted off her bed and into the glow of the lantern. "Surely that will be enough."

◆ ◆ ◆

The rain had stopped during the night. He could hear the river and knew it had risen very high. In the last two months, Paul had seen many things happen in Cerro Verde. After the two Bolivian padres had shown up—both doctors and the right kind of missionaries, there for the long haul—his ordeal took on a momentum all its own. Paul gave the gold bars to Seamus, who returned to Raul and waited anxiously for the old negro and his barge that swung by once a week, luck and monsoon permitting. They chugged back to the Macunaima mine and cashed out the gold, then the two men and the Caboclo kid punished the rust-bucket all the way down to Porto Velho and bought nearly 600 kilos of medical supplies. It rained for three days straight and the barge broke down no less than fifteen times getting back to Raul, but the old negro would accept nothing beyond two canned hams for his work, these owed to a jefe at the tin mine. Seamus and the local Indians had spent the last three weeks shuttling supplies up to Cerro Verde. Paul Hudson was leaving Cerro Verde a lot better off than he found it. And now his head had cleared and he felt an unfamiliar burst of strength. It was the

Indian summer of Paul Hudson's life, and he knew it. Knowing another chance might never come, he'd have to make do with today.

The time had screamed by like a meteor. When he'd gotten on the scale the previous week, and seen he was down to 127 pounds, he realized his meaningful days were over. For the last month, he could manage to stay on his feet only half an hour at a go. The only thing waiting for him was profound sloth and total dependence on the others, who were very busy, and he wouldn't let it come to that.

He stretched back on his cot and pulled out the diary he'd been keeping these last few months. That had been Joao's gift to him, the idea of putting some of his thoughts and feelings into words. In the last month alone he'd filled sixty-eight pages. He grabbed a pen, stretched back on his cot and in a tight, neat hand, made one final entry.

November 1

I know at this very second thousands, even millions of others are clawing up their own steep paths, horrendous, hellish ones,immeasurably worse than mine has ever been. And I marvel at the spirit of the thing, the endless Fact that people will cling to the bleakest creation ever imagined if they've even the slightest hope to someday love something—something meager as an hour's peace, a crust of bread, a bar of gold. Ultimately, I've been one of the lucky ones. And today, I feel especially lucky.

Paul folded the diary and placed it on his cot. He shaved, put on his clean shirt and walked outside.

From the shade of a tree he could see into the clinic, could watch Rafaella, the woman of his gifts, bustling around. She'd been up most of the night with him, watched while his core temperature dropped so low he got convulsive shivers. He'd passed out for three hours and when he woke he was wrapped in blankets, with Rafaella rubbing hot balsam on his temples. Now, fighting the odds in a dirt-floored clinic, she was right where she had to be. It took him nearly an hour, stopping many times, to make his way along the river to the shadow of the green peak. That towering emerald bullet was the first thing he'd encountered there, barely five months before. They said it reached up and up and never stopped, for the summit was forever obscured by clouds, and had never been seen. Paul gazed up at the spire for a last time, and marveled. In a remote jungle, on a lonely desert, in the middle of a city, good men find beauty, weak men find evil.

He stumbled on downstream, his feet slowly but confidently working toward a canoe on whose warped and sun-bleached bones lived the flesh of a universal myth: that anyone who paddled into the roaring gorge below would live forever. This canoe, Paul believed, was the last link in an unbroken chain stretching back into the vault of ages. Every canoe and every traveler varied in substance and form, but in the end all souls paddled into the unknowable gorge.

Paul was almost there. Just to his right the great river ran, winding, thundering, ebbing, flowing, into the ocean of time.